Counseling on
Family Planning and
Human Sexuality

Counseling on
Family Planning
&
Human Sexuality

BARBARA R. BRADSHAW, PH.D.
WALTER McILHANEY WOLFE, JR., M.D.
THERESA J. WOOD, M.S.S.W.
LUCY STANSBURY TYLER, M.D.

Family Service Association of America
New York

Library of Congress Cataloging in Publication Data

Bradshaw, Barbara R.
    Counseling on family planning & human sexuality.

    Includes index.
    1. Birth control. 2. Family social work. 3. Sex
therapy. I. Bradshaw, Barbara R.
HQ766.C638   362.8'2   75–27961
ISBN 0–87304–142–9
ISBN 0–87304–129–1 pbk.

Contents

Acknowledgments

The authors wish to express their deep appreciation for the assistance of the following people: Marjorie Crow and Felicia Guest, associated with the Emory University Family Planning Program and editors of *True to Life*, provided invaluable editorial consultant help. Much of the background work was contributed by graduate students at Kent School of Social Work: Delores Bynum, Phyllis Gateskill, Barry Jacobs, Eric Baker, Jane Huseth, Melinda Foster, and Jean Myers. The latter two made further contributions: Melinda Foster by her expertise in abortion counseling and Jean Myers by seeing the project through to completion. Donald Cooke added his skills as advisor and editor to the final writing stages. Herbert Bisno, Dean, and Dutton Teague, Assistant Dean, Kent School of Social Work, University of Louisville, were consistently helpful and supportive. Elaine Dennison, Ph.D., gave a thoughtful and helpful review of the technical sections. Robert A. Hatcher, M.D., M.P.H., Constance C. Conrad, M.D., M.P.H., Randolph W. Kline, M.D., Gary K. Steward, M.D., Frank L. Moorhead, M.D., and Robert C. Sorensen, Ph.D.

have graciously given permission to reprint tables from their work.

The manuscript was typed with great patience and understanding by Barbara Bush and Sharron McConnell.

Introduction

Social workers should take the professional responsibility to assist clients in obtaining whatever help and information they need for effective family planning. Because in their day-to-day work social workers are knowledgeable about family and community resources, they have many opportunities to help clients obtain desired services. Individual social workers also have a professional obligation to work with a variety of groups on the domestic and international fronts for the establishment of family planning programs on a level adequate to insure the availability and accessibility of family planning services to all who want them.[1]

No profession has tackled the challenges of birth control and human sexuality with any gusto. Even in medical schools, training in human sexuality was unavailable until a few years ago, and many aspects of sexuality and fertility control are not mentioned in most medical textbooks today. Schools of social work are just beginning to incorporate these fields into their curricula.[2]

1. Resolution adopted by the Delegate Assembly of the National Association of Social Workers, 1967.
2. For analysis of the lack of professional attention given to human sexuality and family planning see Naomi Abramowitz, "Human Sexuality

Social workers, however, have been providing family planning and sexual counseling for years, often with little recognition. It has, in fact, become apparent that the social work profession can make major contributions to the provision of birth control services. And social workers are seeing the need for special training and information.

Historically, the only pioneers in the fields of family planning and human sexuality have been isolated individuals, not entire disciplines. The major innovators were labeled as deviants: Margaret Sanger was jailed; Alfred Kinsey endured criticism and pressure from almost every imaginable source; and William H. Masters was asked to resign from the Central Association of Obstetricians and Gynecologists.

Widespread access to effective contraceptives has developed only within very recent history. Oral contraceptives were not approved until 1960, intra-uterine devices were not available until 1964, and no federal money was spent on family planning until 1966. The need for the full range of family planning services, including abortion and voluntary sterilization, was not widely recognized until the late sixties and early seventies, with the rise of a viable women's rights movement. With the exception of limited medical research and rather extensive investments by drug companies, no profession has been committed for any long period of time to family planning.[3]

In little over a decade, the field of family planning has undergone significant changes: a rapid expansion of contraceptive technology; abrupt changes in attitudes and legal barriers to providing family planning services; new awareness of human sexuality as a valid field of study; and recognition of the rights of women to control their own

in the Social Work Curriculum," *The Family Coordinator,* 20 (October 1971), pp. 34–35; and Margaret Burnstein, "Social Work Practice Toward Enhancing Competence in Family Planning," *Perspectives in Social Work,* 2: 1 (New York: Adelphi University School of Social Work, 1968).

3. *Commission on Population Growth and the American Future* (New York: New American Library, 1972), p. 181.

bodies. In spite of these advances, much still needs to be done. The following considerations illustrate the continuing need to provide family planning services.

1. It is estimated that in fiscal year 1972, income factors barred 8.8 million women aged fifteen to forty-four from full access to family planning services, and other access problems affected an additional 8.1 million women.[4]

2. As of 1972, thirteen countries had lower infant mortality rates than the United States. Ten had lower maternal death rates.[5]

3. There are an estimated 10 million malnourished people in America. Forty percent of them are children. Malnutrition in the early years of life retards physical and mental development.[6]

4. Approximately 17 percent of all births are to teenagers. Adolescents are more likely than adults to have premature infants, with the accompanying mortality and morbidity risks.[7]

5. The proportion of out-of-wedlock births with their high risk of prematurity and infant deaths almost doubled among fifteen- to nineteen-year-olds between 1960 and 1968.[8]

6. The 1970 National Fertility Study reports twice the incidence of unwanted births among couples with incomes below $4,000 as among those with incomes of $10,000 or above. Overall, the incidence of unwanted births among *married* couples in 1970 was 33 percent[9] and in 1972, over 200,000 unwanted infants were born to teen-agers.[10]

4. Charlotte Muller, "Fertility Control and the Quality of Human Life," *American Journal of Public Health,* 63:520 (June 1973). There is debate over the extent of the need. The figure is a higher estimate.
5. *New York Times,* March 18, 1973, p. 48.
6. *Commission on Population Growth,* p. 130.
7. Ibid., p. 144.
8. Ibid., p. 145.
9. Leslie Westoff and Charles Westoff, *From Now To Zero* (Boston, Mass.: Little, Brown & Co., 1971), p. 290.
10. Sol Gordon, *Say It So It Makes Sense,* pamphlet, Syracuse University, New York, Winter, 1973, p. 1.

xiv | INTRODUCTION

7. Pregnancy is much more risky than use of contraceptives. The mortality from thromboembolism attributable to the pill is about 3 deaths per 100,000 women per year. The risk of death from pregnancy is about 30 per 100,000 per year or ten times greater.[11]

The needs of the client population, the changes in contraceptive technology, and the recognition of their own abilities and responsibilities in this area have created an urgent need among social workers for up-to-date information about reproductive biology, sexual behavior, and birth control technology. They have also created an accompanying need for greater understanding and objectivity in the highly personal and complicated area of human sexuality.

This book is designed to provide social workers with just such information and awareness. The book is organized into seven major parts. In the first part some of the social realities which the social worker must face are considered, especially contraception and the law, and some consequences of unwanted fertility (unwanted children). In the second part, human sexuality is examined, including physiology and functioning, major sexual problems, teen-age sexuality, and fertility related questions (conception, infertility, and menopause). The third part examines the social worker's role in counseling on family planning and human sexuality, including a discussion of the counselor's sexuality, a sample interview guide, and referral techniques. The fourth part is devoted to sexual counseling with adults: contraceptive counseling; conception, infertility, and genetic considerations; menopause and sexuality; and abortion and sterilization counseling. In part five the focus is on sexual counseling with adolescents, exploring such topics as masturbation, venereal disease,

11. Saja Goldsmith, "Medical Aspects of Family Planning" in Joanna Gorman, ed., *The Social Worker and Family Planning* (Berkley, Calif.: University of California, reprinted Department of Health, Education, and Welfare, 1970).

and homosexuality, among others. Part six provides a detailed discussion of physician-related, non-prescription, and permanent methods of birth control, as well as a description of the abortion techniques that are currently available. Part seven supplies a final note and index.

In preparing this book, we have considered the variety and range of social workers' interests and functions. It is our belief that any social worker can incorporate the information contained here into her particular activities.[12] She may inform clients of the availability and desirability of family planning services and the variety of birth control methods available. She may need to provide accurate and sometimes highly critical and technical information to a client with an unwanted pregnancy; or she may need to counsel or reassure her client about sexual behavior. Frequently, the social worker is the person to whom the client turns for reassurance that medical decisions and recommendations will not be harmful, and the social worker may often help to correct problems of folk misinformation. Some social workers may also help alleviate clients' sexual dysfunctions or interpersonal problems which may interfere with successful contraception.

The counseling issues are highly personal, but the social worker's training and experience regarding many other intimate levels of her client's lives should have prepared her for these responsibilities. The social worker, perhaps more than any other professional, is frequently in a position to help a woman achieve and maintain control over her own reproductive career.

12. Because most social workers and most contraceptive users are women, feminine pronouns are generally used in this book.

I

SOCIAL
PERSPECTIVES

1

The Unwanted Child

The Whites had been married ten years and had five children ranging in age from two to nine when they came to the attention of the authorities. They were reported for gross neglect and abuse of the children. The father was twenty-eight but looked more like forty or forty-five because of his weatherbeaten, wrinkled face and his extremely poor teeth. He worked sporadically as an unskilled laborer, and had been in the habit of drinking heavily since age sixteen. He himself had been physically abused as a child by his father who beat him severely and locked him out of the house all night for disciplinary reasons on numerous occasions.

The mother was twenty-five, but also looked a great deal older. Neither parent had had much education and both had grown up in poverty.

The father and mother had maintained a relationship which alternated between brief periods of caring for each other and more frequent periods of abusing each other. When the father drank and became angry at the mother, he would threaten to kill her and the children with a gun. His anger would reach such proportions that he would pick up the children and slam them against the wall. Although the children were frequently bruised,

3

they had never suffered any broken bones.

Even though the abuse of the children was frequent, the family came to the attention of the authorities only because neighbors reported the mother's neglect of them. She often left the children alone, and did not feed them. The mother herself had been frequently neglected in the same manner. It was during a quarrel that both parents left home and the children were left unattended. Neighbors reported them to the authorities shortly afterwards.

At the time the authorities became involved, the mother had become pregnant again, but before the children were removed from the home she had disappeared. Before her disappearance, the social worker learned that none of the children had been planned, and with each succeeding child the parents' frustration increased. The mother had revealed her complete lack of knowledge regarding birth control. She had come from a large family herself and her own lifestyle was similar to her mother's. She had been pregnant at the time of her marriage, and each pregnancy was looked upon as something that just happened, not something that was planned or even talked about.[1]

An infant has no say about entering the world. His parents often have little more control, especially if they know little about sex and contraception. When conception is viewed as an unfortunate accident, parents are prone to feelings of powerlessness, and any unresolved resentment may be transferred to the child.

The unwanted child is the child whose parents view his existence primarily as a burden. The child is seen as a liability, a restriction to the parents' freedom, and an intruder into their relationship. Defined in primarily negative terms, the unwanted child is likely to act out the role in which he has been cast.

The incidence of unwanted pregnancy among married couples declined from 19 percent during 1960–64 to 15 percent during 1965–70. Improved family planning practices have been credited by some with having helped pre-

1. Representative of typical case material supplied by the Division of Protective services, Kentucky Department of Child Welfare.

vent 750,000 unwanted births between 1966 and 1970.[2] The proportion of unwanted births increases strikingly with birth order. Larry Bumpass and Charles Westoff report that 5 percent of first births by married couples are unwanted, contrasted with 30 percent of fourth births and 50 percent of sixth or higher-order births. Poverty also increases the likelihood that births will not be desired. Fifteen percent of births to non-poor families are unwanted, compared with 23 percent among the near-poor and 37 percent among the poor.[3] Many of these unwanted births have serious negative effects on parents, children, and society.

Whether a child is wanted, is not of course, determined solely on the basis of whether the pregnancy was by plan or by accident. There are some reasons for pregnancy that can negatively affect how the child will be perceived.

Undesirable Motives for Parenthood

Sexual adequacy is a quality that many feel the need to demonstrate, both to themselves and to others. Conceiving children may represent proof of potency or virility, and thus validate the parent's sexual identity. Studies show that this thinking is particularly prevalent among teen-age males and may also be widespread among aging men.[4] In a social system which limits the areas of recognition for women, motherhood is likely to be over-valued. Both men and women in low-income groups may gain a sense of personal security through parenting children.

Adult independence for many is substantiated by parenthood, which may represent a means of competing with

2. Frederick S. Jaffe, "Family Planning Services in the United States," in U.S. Commission on Population Growth and the American Future, Aspects of Population Growth Policy, etc. R. Parke, Jr., and C.F. Westoff, U.S. Government Printing Office, Washington, D.C., 1972.

3. Larry Bumpass and Charles Westoff, "Unwanted Births and U.S. Population Growth," Family Planning Perspectives, 2:9–11 (October 1970).

4. Phyllis Ewer, Atlanta Adolescent Pregnancy Project Evaluation Unit, personal communication, 1972.

their own parents. This psychoanalytic theory suggests that a woman's first child may be an attempt to surpass her mother. The birth resembles an initiation rite, and has symbolic value as an entry into adulthood.

Normalcy is highly valued in our society; some people respond to social pressure to prove their normalcy by marrying and having children. Until recently, a woman who did not desire children was considered abnormal, emotionally ill, or sexually inadequate. Family and peer pressure may also have a tremendous impact on family size; this pressure is now changing in favor of smaller families.

Dependency needs may indirectly influence a decision to have a child; caring for a helpless creature may enhance one's feeling of importance and, thus, a particularly dependent person is likely to be gratified by being depended upon. A parent may project her own needs onto the child and identify with the child so strongly that the parent is actually taking care of herself.

Marital problems often lead to the decision to have a child. Some couples believe that children will save their marriage. Becoming pregnant to resolve differences or to draw the couple together usually means an attempt to obligate one partner to the other. Such bonds are more confining than unifying and seldom benefit problem marriages.

Outside goals may underlie a pregnancy. Out-of-wedlock conception can serve covert purposes. Pregnancy may be a way to obtain a marital partner or to express hostility toward parents or the opposite sex.

People usually have mixed feelings about having children and are frequently unaware of their negative attitudes about parenthood. Some of the reasons for not having children affect how a child conceived accidentally may be viewed.

Reasons for Not Having Children

Personality problems may be aggravated by parenthood because of the time, effort, and patience required for child-rearing. Realizing their limitations, some people prefer not to have children.

Feelings of psychosexual inadequacy may be intense, and insecure people may doubt their ability to be adequate parents. Feelings of doubt may be particularly true of women who view their own mothers as seriously inadequate.

Situational factors may be crucial in the desire not to have children: they may be temporary, such as marital status or educational goals, or they may revolve around a career that consumes a great deal of time and energy and which requires a lifestyle that is not suited to child-rearing. Poor health or the number of children already in the family may be permanent reasons for not wanting to initiate a pregnancy.

Economic considerations are often involved in the desire not to have a child. The United States Department of Labor statistics indicate that a yearly income of $11,446 is required for an average urban family of four to have a modest-to-adequate standard of living.[5] The reason given most frequently for using contraception is economic.[6]

Current concerns over population and pollution, together with a feeling of responsibility to the rest of society, may influence the desire not to have children.

When an unwanted pregnancy does occur, the couple typically experiences shock, disbelief, depression or anxiety (possibly including suicidal thoughts or even attempts), and then most often acceptance. After delivery, when the child's physical reality cannot be denied, renewed feelings

5. Department of Labor, *Minimum Adequate Standard of Living for a Nonfarm Family of Four* (Washington, D.C.: U.S. Government Printing Office, 1973).
6. Charles Westoff, Robert Potter, and Phillip Sagi, *The Third Child: A Study in the Prediction of Fertility* (Princeton: Princeton University Press, 1963).

of rejection of the child and inadequacy as a parent may occur. When feelings of rejection and guilt are repressed parents often become overly protective. They may also place unrealistic demands upon themselves to be perfect parents. Too often the results of such demands are mixed and confusing signals to the child.[7]

The Battered Child Syndrome

A further tragedy of the unwanted child is that he may suffer from physical abuse as well as from psychological abuse. In 1960, the Children's Bureau of the United States Department of Health, Education and Welfare began gathering data from physicians regarding evidence of child battering. Since then, attempts have been made to survey the "Battered Child Syndrome" on a nation-wide basis. The size of the problem has been growing. There were 9,300 cases of reported child abuse for the nation in 1967. In 1968 there were 10,931 reported child abuse cases in the United States.[8] The American Medical Association has called the Battered Child Syndrome the number one cause of early childhood death, and estimates the incidence at 50,000 per year.[9] The highest projected incidence is derived from extrapolation of data from California and Colorado, where careful surveillance is maintained. These data give a conservative estimate of 200,000 to 250,000 children a year in need of protective services because of physical abuse. This rise in the number of incidents is partly due to the increased awareness on the part of physicians, social workers, and others, who are recognizing cases of child abuse and reporting them more often than in the past.[10]

7. David Gil, *Violence Against Children* (Cambridge: Harvard University Press, 1972).

8. Vincent DeFrances, *Child Abuse Legislation in the 1970s* (Denver, Colo.: The American Humane Association, Children's Division, 1970), p. 1.

9. Columbia Broadcasting System, Evening News Report, June 27, 1973.

10. Theo Solomon, "History and Demography of Child Abuse," *Symposium on Child Abuse, Pediatrics Supplement,* 51:755 (June 1971).

Most injuries result from beatings with electrical cords, hair brushes, baseball bats, bottles, television aerials, and fists. Some children have had their feet, hands, and arms deliberately burned on gas burners or with cigarette lighters. Others have been scalded by hot liquids, and some have been stabbed, shot, or thrown violently to the floor. Bruises, contusions, and broken bones are the commonest injuries.[11]

The results of a study conducted by the American Humane Association, indicate that battered children are not confined to one socio-economic stratum, and that religious beliefs have no bearing on whether children are battered. Autistic children, the mentally retarded, the physically handicapped, and hyperactive children are more likely to be battered than are "normal" children.[12]

Alan Guttmacher cites evidence that the abused child is often a product of an unwanted pregnancy which may have begun before marriage, too soon after marriage, or at some other inconvenient time. He notes that in a single family several children may be beaten or only one child may be singled out for abuse because of a specific factor, such as his or her sex.[13]

The Battered Child Syndrome is, of course, not simply the result of unwanted pregnancies. Some people will choose to have children and will later abuse them. A social picture of the abusive parent as well as the abused child can be formulated from the composite demographic description, based on the writings of Theo Solomon, shown in table 1 on the following page.[14]

The unwanted child is a tragic phenomenon. So is unwanted parenthood. Not only should social workers be

11. Vincent Fontana, "The Diagnoses of the Maltreatment Syndrome in Children," *Symposium on Child Abuse, Pediatrics Supplement,* 51:780–82 (June 1971).

12. Ray Helfer, "The Etiology of Child Abuse," *Symposium on Child Abuse, Pediatrics Supplement,* 51:777–79 (June 1971).

13. Alan Guttmacher, "The Tragedy of the Unwanted Child," *Parents Magazine,* June 1964, p. 6.

14. Solomon, "History and Demography of Child Abuse," p. 775.

TABLE 1

A. The abused child

Average age: under four years, most under two.
Average death rate: 5 percent to 25 percent. The highest reported rate is from California; in New York City, substantiated, 5.4 percent; unsubstantiated is 17 percent.
Average age at death: slightly under three years.
Average duration of exposure to battering: one to three years.
Sex differentiation: none.

B. The abusive parent

Marital status: overwhelming majority were married and living together at the time of the abuse.
Average age of abusive mother: 26 years.
Average age of abusive father: 30 years.
Abusive parent: father slightly more often than mother.
Most serious abuse: mother more often than father.
Most common instrument for abuse: hairbrush.

C. Family dynamics

Thirty to 60 percent of abusing parents claim to have been abused as children themselves.
High proportion of premarital conception.
Youthful marriage, often forced.
Unwanted pregnancies.
Illegitimacies.
Forced marriages.
Social and kinship isolation.
Emotional problems in marriage.
Financial difficulty.

concerned about battered children, they should also be responsive to the needs of women who have, or are likely to have, unwanted pregnancies. If social workers are to stop the "unwanted child syndrome," they need to be familiar with contraceptive technology and counseling techniques; these are essential tools in enabling clients to decide their own future.

2

Contraception and the Law

Whatever the rights of the individual to access to contraceptives may be, the rights must be the same for the unmarried and married alike . . . if the right to privacy means anything . . . it is the right of the *individual*, married or single, to be free from unwarranted governmental intrusion into matters so fundamentally affecting a person as the decision whether to bear or beget a child.[1]

As a result of the Supreme Court decision, part of which is quoted above, contraception is now legal for adults in all states. Differences still exist, however, in terms of laws governing ease of access to contraceptives and sterilization—minors are treated differently from state to state. Abortion laws are in flux because of the many unresolved issues following in the wake of the 1973 Supreme Court abortion decisions (Roe v. Wade and Doe v. Bolton).[2]

1. Eisenstadt v. Baird (U.S. Supreme Court, May 30, 1972).
2. "United States Supreme Court Issues Sweeping Decision on Abortion," *Family Planning Population Reporter*, 2:1–5 (February 1973).

This change in precedent and lack of clarity in the law reflects the complexity of the issues surrounding birth control. Although there is some backlash because of the sweeping changes implied in the 1973 abortion decisions, the general direction of legislation and legal decisions is toward increasing the rights of all individuals to have access to the full range of family planning services as a part of their guaranteed rights to privacy and self-determination.

Access to Contraceptives

In light of the 1972 United States Supreme Court ruling, that states could not prevent the sale of contraceptives, individual states have modified their laws so that use of contraceptives is now legal for adults in all states. However, more than half the states retain statutes which, in effect, prohibit or restrict in some way the sale, distribution, or display of contraceptives. About twenty-two states restrict the sale of all or some contraceptives, although all of these states allow exemptions for doctors, pharmacists, or other licensed firms or individuals. Approximately thirty states forbid the advertising of contraceptives and the dissemination of information about them, but almost all make exceptions under certain circumstances.[3] At least twenty-seven states, either expressly or inferentially, prohibit the sale of contraceptives through vending machines.[4]

Teen-agers are often barred access to contraception, not by laws pertaining explicitly to contraception, but by common law restrictions, inconsistent and never universally applied, which pertain to the need for parental consent for minors seeking medical care. Yet, many exceptions are recognized by the same body of common

3. Dienes Thomas, *Law, Politics and Birth Control* (Chicago: University of Illinois Press, 1972), pp. 317–19.
4. Ralph Petrilli, *Legal Aspects of Family Planning Methods*. Report on Family Planning Grant No. 04–H–00458–02–0 (Washington, D.C.: Department of Health, Education, and Welfare, 1973), p. 338.

law, including the sanction of contraceptive services to teen-agers in emergencies or in cases where the minor is married or otherwise "emancipated." Although many exemptions exist, the uncertainty and ambiguity in the general laws governing medical services to minors have made many physicians reluctant to prescribe contraceptives, even for sexually active minors who have been, or who clearly will be, exposed to the risk of pregnancy.

Much of this hesitancy on the part of physicians stems from their fear of encountering lawsuits brought by parents, guardians, or community groups. The fact is that no lawsuit has ever been initiated in an attempt to prohibit either clinics or private physicians from providing contraceptive services for teen-agers.[5] Nevertheless, although there has been some increase in the willingness to serve adolescents, physicians remain cautious. Faced with this reluctance on the part of the medical and related professions, an ever-increasing number of states have enacted new laws to permit minors access to contraceptive devices and information without parental consent. A survey of legislation revealed that twenty-five states had extended to at least certain categories of minors the right to birth control and other pregnancy-related services, and, in some cases, to all forms of medical care.[6]

Sterilization

Voluntary sterilization for both males and females is legal in all states except Utah, if elected by the patient and physician.[7] For married women, the consent of the spouse is also required in most states; in some states the same is true for married men. Unmarried minors must usually

5. Interview with Russel Richardson, Director, Governor's Commission on Family Planning, Georgia, 1973.

6. Harriet Pilpel and Nancy Wechsler, "Birth Control, Teenagers and the Law: A New Look, 1971," *Family Planning Perspectives*, 3:-37–46 (July 1971).

7. Lawrence Lader, ed., *Foolproof Birth Control* (Boston: Beacon Press, 1972), p. 22.

have parental consent, although this requirement is being challenged in the courts. Mentally competent minors when married or otherwise emancipated must often have parental consent in addition to the consent of the spouse. Women who are separated or divorced are often treated as single persons, and the partner's consent is not deemed necessary. Frequently, however, physicians are hesitant to perform voluntary sterilization on a woman without spousal consent, even when the husband cannot be located.[8]

To further cloud the legal issues surrounding sterilization procedures, in recent years there has been a rash of lawsuits brought against hospitals with restrictive sterilization policies by patients requesting sterilization. These suits have challenged policy restrictions on age, number of children, and marital status. To date, the patient's right to obtain sterilization if so desired has been upheld by the courts. No lawsuits against physicians for failing to perform sterilization procedures have been brought to the courts.[9]

Involuntary sterilization for the mentally retarded and mentally ill varies from state to state. In twenty-seven states, sterilization for the mentally incompetent is legal. In these states, an incompetent who meets the statutory requirements may be legally sterilized by following the mandatory procedures outlined in the statutes. In most of these states, a petition for permission to perform sterilization procedures on mentally incompetent persons must be brought to the courts by the legal guardians. In states with no statutes governing involuntary sterilization, legalities must be gleaned from analyses of existing cases of sterilization. In most of these states, involuntary sterilization is allowed by common law precedent.[10]

8. Petrilli, *Legal Aspects of Family Planning Methods,* p. 306.
9. Walter Wolfe, "Female Sexual Sterilization, Medical Progress," *Journal of the Kentucky Medical Association,* 71:91 (February 1973).
10. Petrilli, *Legal Aspects of Family Planning Methods,* pp. 210, 213.

As the result of a $1,000,000 lawsuit brought on behalf of two minors who were sterilized with parental consent but without court petition, the Department of Health, Education and Welfare has developed guidelines regarding sterilization of minors and other legally incompetent persons. In the 1974 District of Columbia case, Relf v. Weinberger, it was held that

> federal funds could not be authorized for sterilization procedures under guidelines which allowed a review committee to sanction the operation without requiring the personal consent of the incompetent. Judge Gerhard Gesell found that the notion of voluntary consent, "at least when important human rights are at stake, entails a requirement that the individual have at his disposal the information necessary to make his decision and the mental competence to appreciate the significance of that information. . . . No person who is mentally incompetent can meet these standards nor can the consent of a representative, however sufficient under state law, impute voluntariness to the individual actually undergoing irreversible sterilization."[11]

Legal Aspects of Abortion

According to Dr. Louis Hellman, former Deputy Assistant Secretary for Population Affairs, Department of Health, Education and Welfare, a separation must be made between family planning, abortion, and other services. Any federal monies used for family planning services must not be spent on abortions or abortion counseling. Abortion counseling and services may, however, be provided within the same program if they are performed by personnel under other funding patterns.[12] Hospital or public welfare social workers, for instance, can provide this

11. Columbia Human Rights Law Review Staff, *World Population Control: Rights and Restrictions* (New York: Family Service Association of America, 1976), p. 159.
12. Louis Hellman (Paper presented at Postgraduate Conference on Family Planning, Department of Gynecology and Obstetrics, Emory University School of Medicine, Atlanta, Georgia, Spring 1972).

counseling, and the hospital staff can perform abortions using Medicaid funds for the medically indigent. Some well-publicized efforts are being made to halt the use of federal funds for abortions, but these bills, if passed, will be tested in the courts and probably declared unconstitutional as discriminatory against the poor.

State and local legislative restrictions may impose limitations on the provision of abortion counseling and services in agency settings, including hospitals and public welfare agencies, but there are no federal stipulations that abortion counseling services cannot be provided by social workers.

On January 22, 1973, the United States Supreme Court ruled on nineteenth century abortion laws in the United States. Its decision will make it necessary for every state in the Union, except possibly New York, which already has liberalized abortion laws, to redefine its abortion laws. The Court stated that the restrictive abortion laws in the United States infringed on the constitutional rights of the impregnated woman—particularly the right to privacy.

The Court held that, prior to the end of the first trimester of pregnancy, the decision to have an abortion "must be left to the medical judgment of the pregnant woman's attending physician." During the second trimester of pregnancy an abortion can be regulated by the state to insure the safety of the woman having the abortion—for example, by requiring that the abortion take place in a hospital. The Court held that because the fetus is viable (can live outside the womb) in the final trimester, abortion can be performed only to save the life or health of the mother. The Court specified that the government's rights supersede the rights of the mother during the last trimester. It remains to be seen whether a constitutional amendment reversing this Supreme Court decision will ever be passed. For the immediate future, abortions will now be more accessible to those women desiring them.

Many legal questions, however, remain unanswered. Paternal rights in general, parental rights in the case of pregnant teen-agers, the legal responsibility of public hospitals to provide abortion services for the indigent, and many other issues will have to be tested in the courts before all of the nuances of the law can be resolved. Thus far, the cases tested in the courts have been largely resolved in the direction of protecting the woman's individual rights.

In the meantime, ironic as it may seem, federal legislation governing all public social service agencies, except for those offering family planning services with federal funds, leaves social workers free to offer abortion counseling and referral services.

Social Workers and the Law

Social workers in public agencies are now required by law to see that their Aid to Families with Dependent Children (AFDC) clients have access to birth control services. In accord with Social Security Amendments of 1967, public welfare workers are mandated by law to discuss family planning services with all AFDC recipients who are in need of such services.

The clear charge of this legislation is that birth control services should be offered to recipients of public assistance. Their continued eligibility for economic aid, however, does not depend on the acceptance of these services, and coercion is not the intent of the law. This provision for birth control services represents a major reversal in public policy, which had previously, either overtly or covertly, opposed efforts to include family planning in the range of services offered to clients receiving public assistance.

Such a major revision is difficult for some older workers and administrators to accept, because the previous assumption had been that recipients of public assistance were, or should be, sexually inactive when husbands were not present in the home.[13] With this legal backing of family planning services, current social work trends are directed

13. Bernard Greenblatt, "Policy Issues on Welfare Referrals to Birth Control Programs," in *Family Planning: Readings and Case Materials*, ed. Florence Haselkorn (New York: Council on Social Work Education, 1971), pp. 34–52.

toward providing the economically deprived with medical access to birth control comparable to that of middle-class women who have access to mainstream medical services.

Teen-agers, if they are recipients of public welfare funds, can also be provided with contraceptive counseling and services by social workers. The law regarding other categories of teen-agers (for example, the mentally ill, the mentally retarded, the delinquent, and so forth) is less clear and more dependent on state and local laws.

Sources of Information on the Legal Aspect of Family Planning

Most questions about local or state laws regarding the legal rights of clients and the responsibilities of professionals can be answered through the local Planned Parenthood Affiliate; the local Legal Aid Society or American Civil Liberties Union Office; or the State Attorney General's Office.

Any questions regarding local or state laws or regulations on both voluntary and involuntary sterilization can be addressed to, The Association for Voluntary Sterilization, National Headquarters, 708 Third Avenue, New York, New York 10017.

In addition to the general resources listed above, legal questions concerning abortions and abortion counseling can be addressed to, The National Organization for Women, Suite 601, 425 13th Street N.W., Washington, D.C. 20004. The Women's Political Caucus, National Headquarters, 1921 Pennsylvania Avenue N.W., Washington, D.C. 20006, or Karen Avery, 2218 Brighten Drive, Louisville, Kentucky 40205; or their local chapters.

II

HUMAN
SEXUALITY

3

Sexual Physiology and Behavior

A young, black mother of four children, pregnant again, told a social worker in an obstretical clinic that she could not accept birth control because it was against her husband's fundamentalist religious principles. It could have ended there with the social worker's acceptance of the fact that she could not challenge religious convictions. However, the social worker responded to the woman's unhappiness about her unplanned pregnancy. Further questioning elicited information about an apparently stable, happy family. Her husband had a steady job, he loved his children and provided well financially for the family. However—and this is a big however—there was a problem because her fear of getting pregnant made her reject his sexual advances frequently and this rejection was the cause of much argument and tension. As she considered what possibilities there were for solving this problem, it gradually became clear to the social worker that the client had a reason why each proposed solution would not work. When the social worker challenged her on this negative attitude, the core problem was finally revealed. She bitterly resented her husband's sexual attitude: "He just comes at me when he wants to. He does not respect me as a person, but that is no reason to leave him. He is a good husband and a good father, so I am stuck.

21

And here I am, pregnant again!" To give her a contraceptive method only would remove her defense and solve nothing. By sticking to her job as a helping person, the social worker was able to peel away the cover story and get to the recognition of the real problem. Had the wife told her husband how she felt? No. They never talked about things like that. With backing from the social worker, the wife finally summoned her courage and talked with her husband about her reaction to his attitudes. To her surprise, he listened and took her seriously. He refused to talk to the social worker, but he did take time off from work, came to the clinic and talked with the doctor. This response was, of course, only the beginning, but it was the beginning of the solution to a serious problem.[1]

Family planners have largely ignored human sexuality as an essential factor in the utilization of contraceptives. Yet, there is a growing awareness, backed by documentation, that sexual attitudes and practices are vital links in controlled, planned fertility. The social worker is often the first to recognize that a client's contraceptive problems are complicated by sexual issues. The development of effective methods of birth control has resulted in the separation of human sexual activity from reproductive behavior. Changes in traditional attitudes toward female sexuality have helped to establish women's right to control their own reproductive careers and to enjoy sexual satisfaction free from reproductive consequences. This chapter presents a review of the current literature on the anatomy and physiology of human sexual functions and responses.

PHYSIOLOGY—MALE AND FEMALE

Male Sexual and Reproductive System
The penis is an external sex organ of the male. It contains three cylinders composed of spongy tissue: two are

1. Miriam Mednick, "The Social Worker's Responsibility in Family Planning," in *The Social Worker and Family Planning*, ed. Joanna Gorman (Berkeley, Calif.: University of California Press, reprinted Department of Health, Education, and Welfare, 1970), p. 56.

cavernous bodies (corpora cavernosa); the third (corpus spongiosum) contains the urethra, which conveys the urine and semen. The head of the penis is known as the glans penis. The glans penis has particular sexual importance because it contains many nerves and is extremely sensitive, particularly at its edges (corona).

A loose fold of skin covering the glans penis is called the foreskin (prepuce). Circumcision removes the foreskin, exposing the glans and usually the corona.

The scrotum is a sac located at the base of the penis which contains male sex glands (testes). The outer skin of the scrotal sac is thick and is somewhat darker than the skin of the rest of the body. The inner layer of skin contains muscle fibers which contract when affected by such stimuli as cold or sexual excitement, causing the scrotum to become heavily wrinkled and elevated. If there is no stimulus, the scrotum hangs loose and its surface is smooth.

The testes (testicles) are a pair of oval, somewhat flattened genital glands (gonads) about one and one-half inches long, located in the scrotum. The testes have two functions: the production of spermatozoa and the secretion of the male sex hormone, testosterone. The left testicle is usually lower and slightly larger than the right testicle.

The epididymis is attached to each testicle. It is a

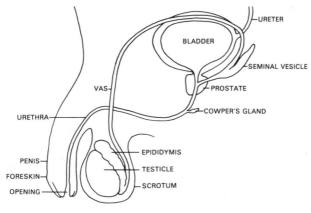

EXTERNAL AND INTERNAL MALE REPRODUCTIVE SYSTEM

tightly coiled series of ducts, through which the sperm are carried to the vas deferens. In the epididymis the sperm develop to final maturation.

The vas deferens, its blood vessels and surrounding tissue, form the spermatic cord attached to each testicle by the epididymis. Each vas deferens extends upward over the pubic portion of the pelvis and into the pelvic cavity. Sperm move from the testes into the epididymis and from there through the vas deferens of the spermatic cord to the ejaculatory duct.

The seminal vesicles primarily function in the storage of sperm and the production of a secretion which is added to the sperm as they enter the ejaculatory ducts. These glands are located at the tip of the vas deferens and are attached to the penile urethra by the ejaculatory ducts.

The Cowper's glands are a pair of glands located on either side of the urethra. During sexual excitement, these tiny glands produce a clear mucous substance which is emptied into the urethra and aids in sperm transport.

The prostate gland is a third gland, located at the base of the bladder. This gland, larger than the Cowper's glands, is about one and one-half inches in diameter. Like the seminal vesicles, it produces a milky substance that accompanies the emission of sperm.

Like the male, the female has both internal and external sexual and reproductive organs. The major reproductive organs of the female, however, are located within the body.

Female Sexual and Reproductive System

The mons pubis is the soft raised area of fatty tissue over the pubic symphysis. At puberty the mons becomes covered with hair and is the most visible part of the female sex organs.

The vulva is the collective term for the external female genitals. The vulva includes the major and minor labia (lips), the clitoris, and the vaginal orifice.

The major lips (labia majora) are two hairy folds of skin that run down posteriorly from the mons pubis. The lips are more prominent in front where they meet. They

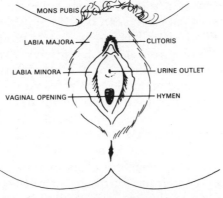

EXTERNAL FEMALE GENITALIA

vary in appearance: some are flat and completely hidden behind the pubic hair; others bulge prominently. Generally the major lips close the genital (pudendal) cleft.

The minor lips (labia minora) are two folds of skin located between the major lips. The upper part, the prepuce, forms a fold of skin over the clitoris. The lower parts meet beneath the clitoris as a separate fold of skin called the frenulum. The space between the minor lips is the vaginal vestibule. The structures enclosed within the minor lips include the clitoris, the external urethral orifice, and the vaginal orifice.

The clitoris is located in front of the urinary opening and consists of two structures of erectile tissue (corpora cavernosa), the tips of which are attached to the pubic bone. The clitoris is endowed with many nerves and is highly sensitive. The clitoris and its attached vestibular bulbs become engorged with blood during sexual excitement, and research indicates that it is the major source of sensation leading to orgasm.[2]

2. The discovery of the clitoris as the locus of sensation leading to orgasm is often thought to be a discovery of the 1960s, although it was occasionally noted in the medical literature earlier. See Robert Dickinson, *Human Sex Anatomy* (New York: Noble Offset, 1947). The credit for bringing the clitoral orgasm to the attention of the general public is often given to Anne Koedt, who wrote "The Myth of the Vaginal Orgasm," *Notes from the New Year,* in 1968. This article has been widely reprinted.

The vaginal orifice is visible when the inner lips are parted. The vaginal orifice can be distinguished from the urethral opening by its larger size and its position in the back of the opening through which urine passes. Appearance of the vaginal orifice, for the most part, depends upon the shape and condition of the hymen. The hymen is a delicate ring-like membrane which usually narrows the vaginal opening. It may surround the vaginal orifice, bridge it, or act as a partial covering. It is usually altered by physical or sexual activity or by childbirth.

The vagina is the recipient of the penis and semen. It also serves as the passage for discharge during menstruation and as the birth canal. In its unaroused state, the vagina is a collapsed muscular tube, not a permanent space. The main surfaces are composed of an anterior and a posterior wall. The anterior wall is longer than the posterior wall. At the upper end, the vaginal canal leads to the cervix. The lower end of the vaginal canal opens into the vestibule between the minor lips. The vaginal wall has few nerves and is a rather insensitive organ.

The uterus or womb is a pear-shaped, muscular, hollow organ, which holds the embryo during pregnancy. The uterus is located behind the bladder and in front of the rectum.

The inner wall of the uterus is lined with a spongy membrane (the endometrium). It consists of many glands and small blood vessels. The endometrial structure varies with the menstrual cycle. The second layer (the myometrium), has intertwining layers of muscle fibers which give the uterine walls great strength and elasticity. The third layer (the perimetrium), is the external cover.

The fallopian tubes are attached on either side of the uterus and extend about four inches between the ovaries and the uterus. At the ovarian end of each tube is a cone-shaped portion (infundibulum), the usual site of fertilization, and tiny finger-like fringed projections (fimbria). The tube opens into the abdominal cavity near the ovary. The

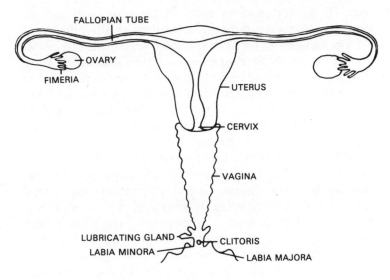

INTERNAL FEMALE GENITALIA (REPRODUCTIVE TRACT)

fallopian tubes assist the movement of the ovum to the uterus by muscular contractions.

The ovaries are small, almond-shaped organs which lie at the back of the ligament on either side of the uterus. The ovaries are held in place by several folds and ligaments. The ovaries have two functions: the release of eggs (ova) and the production of hormones (estrogen and progesterone) which stimulate the endometrium (uterine lining) to grow. It is generally accepted that at birth the ovaries contain all the eggs that will ever be released by the process of ovulation. The immature eggs are contained in tiny groups of cells (follicles).

SEXUAL RESPONSE

The sexual response cycle in both males and females is divided into four phases: the excitement phase; the plateau phase; the orgasmic phase; and the resolution phase. The sexual response cycle described below follows Wil-

liam H. Masters and Virginia E. Johnson's scheme, although information from other sources is also cited.[3]

The excitement phase in the male begins with the erection of the penis. During this phase, the skin of the scrotum begins to thicken and the scrotal sac draws closer to
the body. The spermatic cords shorten, causing a partial
elevation of the testes. The excitement phase may go
quickly into the plateau phase or may last longer depending upon a variety of stimuli.

Vaginal lubrication is the first sign of excitement in the
female. Observable response is confined to the deepest
two-thirds of the vagina. During this phase, the vaginal
barrel lengthens and expands, primarily due to the elevation of the uterus. Both the glans and the shaft of the
clitoris may swell as a result of vascular engorgement.

The plateau phase in the male is when the penis continues to increase slightly in diameter. The testes enlarge
by as much as 50 percent of their unstimulated size, but
because of their elevation they may appear smaller. This
elevation continues, and the skin of the scrotum becomes
even thicker. A clear mucous secretion from the Cowper's
glands may appear in the urethral opening. The amount
is variable and may contain sperm, particularly if there has
been a recent ejaculation.

Of primary importance in the female during this phase
is the formation of the orgasmic platform, as a result of
increased engorgement of the vaginal veins and increased
pelvic muscle tension. At this time, the outer third of the

3. Most of this discussion is based on the findings presented in William H. Masters and Virginia E. Johnson, *Human Sexual Response* (Boston: Little Brown & Company, 1966). Other books on the subject of
sexual functioning are largely interpretations or applications of the Masters and Johnson research. See for example, American Medical Association Committee on Human Sexuality, *Human Sexuality* (Chicago:
American Medical ssociation, 1972); Fred Belliveau and Lin Richter,
Understanding Human Sexual Inadequacy (New York: Bantam Books,
1970); Ruth Brecher and Edward Rays Brecher, eds., *An Analysis of
Human Sexual Response* (New York: Signet Books, 1966); and Herant
Katchadourian and Donald Lunde, *Fundamentals of Human Sexuality*
(New York: Holt, Rinehart and Winston, 1975).

vagina narrows by as much as a half, squeezing the penis. The uterus continues to elevate and may increase in size. The clitoris retracts from the vaginal entrance and its shaft shortens, becoming even more sensitive and tender. Both the labia majora and labia minora increase in size, and there is a marked reddening of the labia minora and vaginal opening.

The orgasmic phase in the male begins with a series of muscular contractions throughout the entire genital area. Just prior to the onset of orgasm, the male first senses an impending ejaculation. After this reaction, at the point of ejaculatory inevitability, the male can no longer control the ejaculatory process. The urethral bulb and the penile urethra undergo rhythmic contractions, which expel the seminal fluid from the penis.

Prior to orgasm, the female experiences a heightening of muscular tension, which indicates that orgasm is imminent. If effective stimulation continues and no distractions occur, orgasm follows. Orgasm begins with waves of sensation and rhythmic contractions of the pelvic muscles. Contractions have been measured in the uterus and outer third of the vagina or orgasmic platform, but orgasmic sensation also occurs in other parts of the pelvic area, particularly in or near the clitoris. Subsequent orgasms may produce either more diverse or more localized rhythmic contractions.

In both sexes there are marked increases in the pulse rate, respiration, and blood pressure, and the sex flush (a physiologic reaction of expansion of blood vessels on the skin surface) becomes widespread. There is a marked increase in general body muscle tension, even in the hands and feet, where spasms may occur. Involuntary pelvic thrusting, sweating, and moaning are common during orgasm.

The resolution phase in the male takes place in two stages. The first stage is a rapid but incomplete loss of erection. The second stage, during which the penis returns to its normal, unexcited size, lasts longer. The time it takes for complete resolution is generally related to the amount of time the male was in the excitement and plateau phases. During this time the testicles descend, and the scrotum thins out and relaxes.

After orgasm, the male goes through a refractory period, during which he is usually unable to have another erection or to ejaculate. The refractory period varies in elapsed time with individuals and circumstances, but it increases with age.

The basic change that takes place in the female during resolution is the gradual loss of the separation and elevation of the labia majora and labia minora. The clitoris returns to its normal positon, the vagina barrel loses its expansion, and the uterus descends. The resolution phase is usually completed within half an hour. Unlike the male, the female requires no refractory period, and some women experience multiple, successive orgasms if stimulation is continued.

A sexually satisfying relationship may be reached without orgasm for both partners. The following five essential conditions are important, however, if both the man and the woman are to experience orgasm: interest on the part of both partners; the reasonably good health of both partners; lubrication of the vaginal walls and erection of the penis; continuation of effective stimulation; and the absence of distracting stimuli.

4

Common Sexual Problems

Mrs. F had not been orgasmic before marriage. In marriage she was orgasmic on several occasions with manipulation but not during coition. As the personal friction between the marital partners increased, she found herself less and less responsive during active coital connection. There was occasional orgasmic success with manipulation. Pregnancy intervened at this time, distracting for a year, but thereafter her lack of coital return was distressing to her and most embarrassing to her husband. He worried as much about his image as a sexually effective male as he did about his wife's levels of sexual frustration. Mrs. F's lack of effective sexual response was considered a personal affront by her uninformed husband.

They consulted several authorities on the matter of "her" sexual inadequacy. The husband always sent his wife to an authority to have something done to or for her. The thought that the situation might have been in any measure his responsibility was utterly foreign to him.[1]

---

1. William H. Masters and Virginia E. Johnson, *Human Sexual Inadequacy* (Boston: Little Brown & Company, 1970), p. 243.

Sexual problems are a common source of psychic and physical suffering. There are times when these dysfunctions and the stresses that they produce are related to difficulties with birth control.

Male Dysfunctions

Among men, the primary dysfunctions are impotence (primary and secondary), premature ejaculation, and ejaculatory incompetence.[2]

Primary impotence is the term used to describe the condition of a man who has never been able to have an erection for purposes of sexual intercourse. It is relatively rare, and is usually associated with multiple etiologies, including severely inhibitory influences in early child development. These factors are frequently compounded by a high anxiety level imposed by religious orthodoxy, involvement in homosexuality, or feelings of inferiority resulting from early sexual experience with overly aggressive or impersonal partners.

Secondary impotence refers to a pattern characterized by an inability to maintain an erection, although the man has experienced successful sexual intercourse at least once in the past. Secondary impotence is far more common than primary. Under certain circumstances, many men exhibit impotence related to anxiety, fatigue, alcohol ingestion, and so forth. These cannot properly be labeled dysfunctions unless a pattern of repeated impotence is established.

Premature ejaculation (orgasm before or immediately after penile-vaginal contact) is the most common sexual dysfunction of men. The condition may or may not be associated with failure of erection. Isolated episodes of premature ejaculation are not uncommon in situations of extreme sexual tension, especially in young men undergo-

2. Discussion of the male dysfunctions is based primarily on Masters and Johnson, *Human Sexual Inadequacy.* As noted in the preceding chapter, other analyses are based in large part on the Masters and Johnson research.

ing initiation to sexual activity. These cannot be labeled as dysfunctions unless a pattern of repeated failure emerges.

Premature ejaculation in the male often affects the female partner. It is a frequent factor in the development of sexual dysfunctions, even pelvic pain, in women. In fact, the problem of premature ejaculation frequently first comes to the attention of the physician when the female partner seeks help because of physical symptoms.

Ejaculatory incompetence is a rare sexual dysfunction in the male, characterized by the inability to ejaculate during vaginal coitus. Males suffering from this dysfunction do not have erectile problems, and are capable of carrying on vaginal intercourse for prolonged periods of time. In initial stages, this ability may be quite satisfactory to the female partner; many women become multiorgasmic under these circumstances. Many females feel, however, that they have "failed" if they are unable to bring their partner to ejaculation; in addition, failure to ejaculate will, of course, result in the inability to conceive. Either of these problems may result in female dissatisfaction, which in turn will be transmitted to the male. Because of his inability to ejaculate, the male may become more or less uninterested in vaginal intercourse, to the point that such activity will become a "chore" rather than an enjoyment. If the female partner pressures the man by demanding ejaculation, then impotence may become a secondary result of this disorder; commonly in such cases, however, the man is able to ejaculate with auto manipulation or with other partners.

As in other sexual dysfunctions, ejaculatory incompetence may be either primary or secondary. The category of primary ejaculatory incompetence includes those males who have never been able to ejaculate during vaginal containment. These men are often individuals with rigid religious standards concerning sexual activity which were formed at a very early age. Secondary ejaculatory incompetence occurs when a normally ejaculatory male loses the ability to ejaculate during vaginal containment.

This phenomenon may be the result of a psychosexual trauma or a change in the man's relationship with his sexual partner; as a result, the male may subconsciously withhold ejaculation. Treatment is difficult, and the results are usually not satisfactory.

This disorder should not be confused with the normal reduction of ejaculatory demand which occurs in men over fifty. In this case there is a normal alteration of male ejaculatory control, in which the man may be capable of long-term, enjoyable maintenance of plateau phase sexual response, though perhaps without ejaculation with each coital experience. It does not mean that he cannot and does not ejaculate, but ejaculation may occur only once in every two or three coital experiences.

The uninformed partner may feel threatened by her inability to bring the male to ejaculation, and may not understand that because of reduction in ejaculatory demand and increased ejaculatory control the male may forego ejaculation in a specific coital connection. The male is able to achieve and maintain full erection almost indefinitely under these circumstances, but will only achieve ejaculation when he himself deems ejaculatory release necessary.

Female Dysfunctions

Among women, the major sexual problems are primary and secondary orgasmic dysfunctions, vaginismus, and pain during intercourse.[3]

Primary orgasmic dysfunction is the term used to describe the condition of a woman who has never experienced orgasm by any method of stimulation—intercourse, masturbation, or manual or oral manipulation of sex organs by a partner. Secondary orgasmic dysfunctions are known as situational orgasmic dysfunctions. These include: masturbatory orgasmic dysfunction (the

3. Discussion of the female sexual dysfunctions is based primarily on Masters and Johnson, *Human Sexual Inadequacy.*

ability to have orgasm with intercourse but not with other kinds of stimulation); coital orgasmic dysfunction (the ability to have orgasm only when induced by masturbation or manual or oral genital stimulation by a partner, but not with intercourse); and random orgasmic dysfunction (orgasm has been achieved at least once in the past but regardless of method of stimulation, orgasm has rarely been accomplished). Another form of coital orgasmic dysfunction is caused by vaginal anesthesia, resulting from the irritation and itching of chronic vaginitis. With this condition, due to a previous vague discomfort, some women cut off all feeling during intercourse, which prevents their achieving any sexual release. This situation is overcome by treating the condition of vaginitis.[4]

Vaginismus is a condition of involuntary, reflex spasms of the muscles around the vaginal entrance. The spasms make it extremely difficult to insert a penis, speculum, or finger into the vagina. Vaginismus is most often caused by repeatedly painful or traumatic intercourse, and may be physical or psychological in origin. It is a learned response which may require specialized therapy even after the original cause has been successfully removed. The condition can be diagnosed only through a physical examination.

Dyspareunia, or pain during intercourse, can be organic or psychological in origin. The pain usually results from lack of lubrication in the vagina. There are three types of dyspareunia: pain on entry; pain during intercourse; and pain after intercourse. Post-coital pain is often the result of pelvic congestion, a condition caused by sexual stimulation without adequate orgasmic release.

Men may also suffer from dyspareunia for various reasons, ranging from allergies or infections to physical abnormalities.

4. Phillip Sarrel (Workshop presentation, Workshop on Human Sexual Behavior, Human Relations Institute, University of Cincinnati, Cincinnati, Ohio, May 7–9, 1973).

Sexual aversion is a psychic phenomenon found in both men and women. Characterized by rejection of all sexual contact, it is a behavior generally learned in one's early home environment or as the result of traumatic sexual experiences. Individuals who have this disorder experience moderate to severe anxiety in situations of a sexual nature. Reactions range from mild fear to acute mental illness.

Treatment

It is easy to assume that sexual dysfunctions are caused by psychological problems. However, a correct diagnosis and treatment of physical conditions and an appropriate discussion of sexual histories can often relieve partners of guilt, blame, and feelings of rejection. Often a purely psychological approach is more problematic, more complex, and counterproductive to the goals of self-acceptance and spontaneity so necessary for sexual adjustment.[5]

Treatment for sexual dysfunctions ranges from fairly simple advice and self-help to highly specialized medical procedures and lengthy therapy. The social worker should neither dismiss a problem nor attempt to go beyond her competence. Although it is the responsibility of the social worker to help the client understand both the environmental and psychological influences and experiences that have produced negative feelings and attitudes, specific problems of sexual dysfunctioning require specialized help. In such cases, a referral should be made to another professional. Sexual counseling is a new, specialized field of practice, and social workers, as well as physicians and psychologists, are increasingly receiving advanced training in this area. Their help should be sought whenever possible.

5. American Medical Association Committee on Human Sexuality, *Human Sexuality* (Chicago: American Medical Association, 1972).

III

THE SOCIAL
WORKER'S ROLE

5

The Counselor's Sexuality

The repeated exercise of submitting subjective involvements to examination and analysis and the accumulated experience of sharing human want and anguish and passions begin to make it possible to take the impact of relationships with greater equilibrium. This is in no sense a "hardening" process. It is rather a mellowing process in which knowledge and acceptance of the differences among human beings, including ourselves, and security as to our professional purposes and capacities serve to steady and temper our emotional responses.[1]

In 1948, Alfred Kinsey stated that social workers have done more sexual counseling than physicians; in 1970, William H. Masters referred to social work as one of the four professions that have treated 75 percent of the sexual problems not treated by the medical profession.[2] In spite of this involvement with sexual counseling, social workers

1. Helen Harris Perlman, *Social Casework: A Problem-Solving Process* (Chicago: University of Chicago Press, 1964), p. 83.
2. Alfred Kinsey, *Sexual Behavior in the Human Male* (Philadelphia: W. B. Saunders Company, 1948), p. 387; and William H. Masters, "Repairing the Conjugal Bed," *Time*, May 25, 1970.

have received little specialized training, and have only recently expressed interest in contraception and human sexuality.[3] It is likely that workers may feel ill-equipped to help the many clients who present contraceptive and sexual problems.

Social workers are as handicapped as most members of society, in that their attitudes and knowledge of sex are highly personal and subjective rather than professional and objective.[4] Like everyone else, social workers have accumulated most of their information and attitudes about sex from their own social experiences and from the mass media. This situation is likely to leave a social worker relatively uninformed about recent sexual and contraceptive research, and too unaware of her own sexuality and its problems and ramifications to be of real help to clients.

Although the social worker has been taught that the focus of counseling begins with the client, it is important that she examine her own attitudes and feelings before beginning to deal with the client's problems. This advice is particularly important when dealing with sexual aspects of a client's difficulties, which can reactivate within the counselor unresolved feelings or conflicts which have lain dormant. When a client presents a problem that is either distressingly similar to, or uncomfortably different from, the counselor's own, it is easy for her to respond with

3. Naomi R. Abramowitz reports that courses in human sexuality did not appear in social work curricula until 1969, "Human Sexuality in the Social Work Curriculum," *The Family Coordinator,* 20:349–54 (October 1971). Only two articles related to family planning appeared in the social work literature between 1950 and 1965. Between 1965 and 1967, only thirteen family planning articles are listed among two thousand classified in National Association of Social Workers abstracts (Margaret Burnstein, "Social Work Practice Toward Enhancing Competence in Family Planning," in *Family Planning, The Role of Social Work, Perspectives in Social Work,* vol.2 (Garden City, N. Y.: Adelphi University School of Social Work, 1968).

4. This situation has been verified in two reports by Florence Haselkorn: "Value Issues for Social Work in Family Planning," in *Family Planning, The Role of Social Work, Perspectives in Social Work,* pp. 7–18; and "Family Planning: Implications for Social Work Education," *Journal of Education for Social Work,* 6:195–98 (Fall 1970).

moralizing, intellectualizing, or silence; to omit relevant questions; or to give inadequate or inappropriate information because of her own anxiety. At the least, an emotional climate may be created that will limit the client's ability to absorb or to use the information presented. To avoid these dilemmas, it is essential that the worker examine and become comfortable with her own sexual values and behavior before attempting to help her clients. This examination might begin with some thoughts about the sources of the worker's own attitudes and assumptions about contraception, parenthood, femininity, and masculinity.

Social workers frequently come from a segment of the population that has been heavily indoctrinated with the romantic, idealized concept of love, which finds sex acceptable only when one is "carried away." Like their clients, some social workers may find it difficult to accept planned sexual behavior, especially when it occurs outside of marriage. The social worker's reaction to planned, "unromantic" sex may range from a vague discomfort, which discourages the client from confronting her own need for contraception, to a direct or subtle rejection of the individual who openly and deliberately anticipates sexual intercourse by using contraceptives. Problems in sexual functioning continue to be labeled as psychiatric illnesses. Such adherence to the medical model by social workers perpetuates unnecessary rejection and negative reactions to behaviors which are not necessarily pathological.

For many people, orthodox religion appears to be a hindrance to sexual adjustment. William H. Masters and Virginia E. Johnson have found that feelings and attitudes based on orthodox religious teachings interfere with normal sexual functioning more than any other factors.[5] Negative feelings about the body have a long tradition, and a strong taboo against viewing and handling the sexual organs still exists for many people. This taboo not only inter-

5. William H. Masters and Virginia E. Johnson, *Human Sexual Inadequacy* (Boston: Little, Brown & Company, 1970).

feres with sexual enjoyment, but may prevent the acceptance or correct use of contraceptive methods which require touching the genitals. It is understandable that social workers, who frequently come from middle-class, religious homes, also have some of these repressive, antisex attitudes. Education should help to change these feelings and attitudes; unfortunately, many educational experiences only compound the problem.

Even before the social work student begins her professional education, she is handicapped by the limitations of the two vocabularies she has been taught to use when talking about sex organs and behaviors. Usually, her socialization has taught her the vernacular of her subculture and persuaded her of its unacceptability. Her formal education may have provided some scientific terms, but it is unlikely that she often uses them outside the classroom. As a result, her vocabulary of anantomical terms is either formal and awkward or slang and inappropriate for serious communication. By the time the social worker begins her professional education, she has probably recognized the inadequacies of both sexual vocabularies. The social work curricula perpetuates this dichtomy in sexual terminology. If slang words are even introduced, it is within the context of an academic discussion of the client's vocabulary, and a negative value judgment is attached. Socially acceptable terms are expected, but the ability to avoid using any terms is the strongest and most effective lesson taught the social work student.

Even if the social worker should become comfortable using a variety of sexual terms, she will often find it difficult to know what to say. Almost nothing is written on the techniques of sexual or contraceptive counseling with low-income clients. There is a dearth of material appropriate to the lower-middle-class and lower-class reader, in spite of the recent popularity of books on sex and marriage. The social worker who tries to learn only through books which appeal to the educated and sophisticated will compound the communication problems already existing between herself and her clients from a lower socioeconomic class. Such books may seem objective and liberal to upper-middle-class readers, but will have little or no value to clients whose lifestyles are more constricted.

The social worker who overcomes the obstacles of inadequate language and content and who learns what to say and how to say it may still be troubled with the problem of her image to the client. Because of the institutional settings in which social workers often practice, workers are frequently identified with the establishment. The result is that a client may anticipate that the social worker will function with the same inhibitions and judgmental attitudes that the client has previously encountered in such agencies.

Social workers are occasionally concerned about jeopardizing their professional and private reputations if their contraceptive and sexual counseling is interpreted as vicarious enjoyment or prurient interest. The real problem arises, however, when anxiety over such a possibility causes the social worker to be vague or to give inappropriate or insufficient emphasis to material that she wishes to cover. It is important that she be comfortable with her own feelings and convey that comfort in a way that frees her clients to accept and respect their own feelings and behavior.

Until the social worker has come to terms with her own sexuality and has accepted her own sexual lifestyle, she cannot be comfortable in permitting others to choose their own. Free from the need to proselytize the client for a particular sexual orientation, she must convey a sense of security and ease with the sexual lifestyle she has chosen. Perhaps the most important message she transmits is her respect for the individuality of the client in determining his or her sexual goals.

6

Interview Guide for Data Base

The following questionnaire is a tool for obtaining the information necessary for contraceptive and sexual counseling and referral. It is designed to cover basic data needs, without eliciting the highly detailed information which may be necessary for certain types of counseling (such as abortion and infertility counseling).

Because the authors believe that social workers should be primarily concerned with obtaining information which will be used in the counseling relationship, an extremely detailed sexual history is not recommended or included here, although at times it may be necessary for the worker to ask more explicit questions when doing in-depth counseling. A detailed guide to evaluation of sexual performance can be found in *Human Sexuality,* a book prepared by the American Medical Association.[1]

Clearly, not all the information requested in this guide is needed for all clients, but the guide should serve as a

1. American Medical Association Committee on Human Sexuality, *Human Sexuality* (Chicago: American Medical Association, 1972).

base for workers as they choose selectively to match individual situations. The goal is to get an accurate picture of all of the client's present activities which may enhance or hinder her use of contraception. A side benefit is that information obtained from this form may be useful in establishing rapport and in providing assistance in other areas. Clients want to talk about themselves, and experience has shown that the use of an interview guide can open the door to communication about many problems.

DATA BASE

Date   Interview Guide: Contraceptive-Sexual History

1. Name _____

2. Date of Birth _____

3. Sex _____

4. Race _____

5. Age at first menstrual period _____

6. Age at first intercourse _____

7. Age at first pregnancy _____

8. Number of living children _____

9. Number of pregnancies _____

10. Marital Status

_____ Married, living with spouse

_____ Unmarried, living with sexual partner

_____ Unmarried, not living with sexual partner

_____ Separated

_____ Divorced

_____ Widowed

11. Years of school completed _____

12. Source of income

_____ Self-employment

_____ Spouse

_____ Both employed

_____ Welfare

_____ Other (please specify) _____

13. a. Have contraceptive services ever been sought?

    _____ Yes

    _____ No

    _____ N.A. (Not ascertainable, not applicable)

  b. (If yes) From whom?

    _____ Planned Parenthood clinic

    _____ Public clinic

    _____ Private doctor

    _____ Other (please specify) _____

14. Method(s) of contraception (check all methods currently used in first column and all methods used in the past in second column).

a. Present	b. Former
_____ Oral medication	_____ Oral medication
_____ IUD	_____ IUD
_____ Condom	_____ Condom
_____ Spermacides (foam, cream, jellies, suppositories)	_____ Spermacides (foam, cream, jellies, suppositories)
_____ Injection (Depo Provera)	_____ Injection (Depo Provera)
_____ Diaphragm	_____ Diaphragm
_____ Withdrawal	_____ Withdrawal
_____ Rhythm	_____ Rhythm
_____ None	_____ None
_____ Sterilized	_____ Sterilized
_____ Currently pregnant	_____ Other (please specify)
_____ Other (please specify)	_____
_____	

15. Is client satisfied with present method of contraception?

_____ Yes

_____ No

_____ Partially satisfied

_____ Wants to try another method

_____ Not applicable

16. Problems associated with current method(s) of contraception
(Probe for physical or psychosocial problems.)

_____

_____

_____

17. Reason for discontinuation of past methods.
(Probe for physical or psychosocial problems.)

_____

_____

_____

18. Any known physical conditions, problems, or disabilities which might
affect use of particular contraceptive methods.

_____

_____

_____

19. Can client and partner discuss use of contraception openly with each
other?

_____ Yes

_____ No

_____ Occasionally

_____ Not applicable

_____ Other (please specify) _____

_____

20. Does partner object to the use of contraception?

_____ Yes

_____ No

_____ To certain methods

_____ Not applicable

21. a. Which method(s) of contraception is preferred by client?

_____

b. Which method of contraception is preferred by partner?

_____

22. Can client and partner discuss feelings about sex freely with each other?

_____ Yes

_____ No

_____ About some things, not others

_____ Not applicable

_____ Other (please specify) _____

_____

23. a. Has assistance with sexual problems ever been sought?

_____ Yes

_____ No

_____ N.A. (Not ascertainable, not applicable)

b. (If yes) Was it obtained?

_____ Yes

_____ No

_____ Not applicable

_____ From whom (please specify) _____

24. Frequency of intercourse (average)

_____ None

_____ Less than once a month (please specify) _____

_____ Once or twice a month

_____ Once a week

_____ Two to four times a week

_____ Five or more times a week

25. Does the client have problems with any of the following?

_____ Techniques of petting and foreplay

_____ Pain associated with intercourse

_____ Does not achieve orgasm

_____ Partner has difficulty obtaining erection

_____ Partner has orgasm too quickly

_____ Fear of pregnancy

_____ Partner wishes more frequent sexual activity than client

_____ Client wishes more frequent sexual activity than partner

_____ Fatigue

_____ Lack of privacy

_____ Interference with sex due to working hours (for example, night work of one partner)

_____ Different attitudes toward sex (please specify) _____

_____

_____ Other (please specify) _____

_____

_____ No problems

26. Are there any interferences with sexual activity due to:

_____ Pregnancy

_____ Separation not due to marital conflict

_____ Separation due to marital conflict

_____ Marital conflict without separation

_____ Health of client or partner

_____ Interference from parents or others

_____ Presence of children

_____ Alcoholism

_____ Family crisis

_____ Psychological problems of client or partner

_____ Other sexual partners

_____ None at present

_____ Other (please specify) _____

_____

_____ Not applicable

27. History of venereal disease

_____ None

_____ Yes; treated

_____ Yes; not treated

_____ Not sure

_____ Not ascertainable

28. History of abortion

_____ Number of spontaneous abortions

_____ Number of induced abortions

_____ legal

_____ illegal

Date of last abortion

_____ spontaneous

_____ induced

29. Number of future pregnancies desired _____

When next pregnancy desired _____

30. Comments

_____

_____

_____

7

Techniques for Successful Referrals

Mrs. B, a pregnant patient in a hospital prenatal clinic, discussed her concern about having any more children. After a considerable amount of discussion, she decided with her doctor that she would have an intrauterine device (IUD) inserted. The doctor told her to come to the family planning clinic the first time she menstruated after she had her baby. The social worker saw her in the hospital during her post-partum stay and said, "If you run into any problem, get in touch with me." I am sure she said it routinely, because she felt that this patient was quite firm in her decision and clear about what she wanted to do. Two months later she heard from her puzzled patient. The problem was that the family planning clinic met only on Wednesday mornings and the patient had begun to menstruate on Thursday. The social worker and Mrs. B figured out that it would be five more months before her menstrual cycle coincided with clinic hours. Mrs. B asked, "What do I do in the meanwhile? Stop living?"[1]

1. Miriam F. Mednick, "The Social Worker's Responsibility in Family Planning," in *The Social Worker and Family Planning*, ed. Joanna Gorman, (Berkeley, Calif.: University of California Press, reprinted Department of Health, Education, and Welfare, 1970), p. 54.

Making successful referrals is an important skill often underrated in the helping professions. The above incident points up some of the problems of referral. Had the social worker been thoroughly familiar with the clinic before making the referral, she would have realized the time limitations and the consequent inaccessibility of that particular service. Knowledge of other family planning clinics in the area would have allowed her to make a more appropriate referral. In addition, more communication with the patient and the post-partum ward staff would have assured that the patient was supplied with and willing to use such interim forms of contraception as foam and condoms. Perhaps special arrangements to provide Mrs. B with an intra-uterine device (IUD) could have been made. On a broader level, the social worker should perhaps work with clinic personnel to arrange more flexibility in hours to increase the availability of services. These considerations highlight the fact that referrals are essentially a social work function, involving the ability to work with a wide variety of service providers, as well as with individual clients.

In general, personnel of family planning clinics are concerned people who are committed to providing accurate birth control information, education, and methods to all women—single or married, young or mature. They are also concerned with patient followup, and appreciate the help of other professionals. By working with family planning staff, a social worker can help motivate a sexually active client to obtain birth control services and to use the methods she chooses.

Before making a referral, the social worker should be familiar with family planning programs in the community. This familiarity should include knowledge of available services, the attitudes of family planning personnel toward clients, clinic procedures, and the amount of time a client will probably have to spend to receive services. Additionally, the social worker should be aware of any problems of eligibility or cost that might affect her client. The ideal way to obtain such information is by visiting family planning clinics in person. If this step is not possible, a telephone call and a request for printed material may be enough to establish a personal contact and to obtain the necessary information.

Making the Referral

Resistance. Motivating clients to use birth control should not imply coercion. The worker should be careful to determine whether the client desires family planning services. She should avoid all judgement, coercion, or implied threats of reprisals if the client does not want to use birth control. Besides being unethical, it is counterproductive, because pressure has a tendency to prevent the kind of commitment which is necessary for a woman to be a successful contraceptor. The following case typifies a common situation:

> Miss H had been referred for family planning services by her public assistance worker because she had just given birth to her fourth illegitimate child and was described as sexually active. She had answered questions regarding previous use of contraception as briefly as possible. She was extremely quiet as she listened to the counselor's explanation and illustration of the various methods of contraception. As she showed no initiative about asking questions and did not respond to encouragement, the worker realized that she was quite hostile and resistant. The worker, therefore, verbalized her understanding that Miss H had feelings about the situation that no one had recognized, and she encouraged her to express them. Miss H admitted that she had not wanted to come but had done so in fear that her Aid to Families with Dependent Children (AFDC) grant would be jeopardized. The worker assured her that this was not so and that she was free to accept or reject contraceptive advice. Miss H refused to believe this; she said that the worker did not understand and that she knew of other AFDC recipients who had lost their grants when they refused to follow through on the referral to the family planning service.
>
> The worker accepted Miss H's concern and again re-

peated her understanding that this was not the policy. She offered to speak to the AFDC worker again to clarify things for both of them. She also explained that this would help Miss H make her own decision as to whether she wanted to use contraception. The worker supported Miss H's right to choose and expressed her hope that Miss H would trust her enough to continue exploration of the problem with her until she had sufficient information to make a decision that was best for her. Miss H seemed relieved and agreed to come again, but gave no indication that she would accept contraceptive use. The worker did not refer to this subject again because she realized Miss H needed time to recognize the real basis of her resistance and then reach a point of sufficient acceptance in subsequent sessions so that she could determine her own wishes about birth control.

In this case, failure to "hear" and correctly interpret the client's silence could have resulted in her long-lasting rejection of any type of contraceptive services.

Ambivalence. Because the client generally makes her own appointment with the doctor or clinic, the social worker can be helpful by providing information about clinic locations, hours, procedure, eligibility, and costs. As the following case demonstrates, the social worker can be supportive by listening to the client's specific problem, concerns, and questions, as well as any ambivalent feelings she may have about birth control and human sexuality.

Mrs. C's husband had consistently refused to assume any responsibility for contraception, and she had had to seek help from the family planning agency the previous year. She had reacted with painful headaches to the pill, rejected the IUD, and decided to use a diaphragm. She became pregnant for the second time soon afterwards.

Because her baby was now two months old and the other child only a year older, she was extremely concerned about becoming pregnant again. She expressed a complete lack of confidence in any form of contraception. She was now refusing to have sexual relations with her husband and was afraid he would turn to another woman as he had been threatening to do. She requested a tubal ligation, and the worker explained medical policy against this procedure for her situation. The worker reviewed all current methods of contraception, but Mrs. C would not even listen to the information. The worker then realized how ambivalent she was. She took considerable time to let Mrs. C know she understood her situation, her conflicted feelings, and the many problems she was attempting to handle at this time. She encouraged Mrs. C to verbalize her feelings. Mrs. C finally expressed her anger toward her husband for his irresponsibility, her disappointment in the use of contraception, and her fear and anxiety about becoming pregnant again. At the end of the interview, the worker offered to have the doctor at the clinic examine Mrs. C so that she would have this additional opportunity to ask questions, to discuss the contraceptive alternatives in-depth, and to learn about her own contraceptive problem. This idea seemed to help Mrs. C, although she sarcastically referred to waiting another month. The worker called to see when the earliest appointment with the doctor could be arranged and learned that Mrs. C could be seen that afternoon because several appointments had been cancelled. Mrs. C began to feel more hopeful and asked the worker to continue to help her. She was assured of this continued support.

A supportive attitude toward the client's desire for effective birth control will encourage the client to believe in her ability to make her own decisions.

Confidentiality. Because many family planning clinics send out postcard reminders to patients about pending or missed appointments, the subject of confidentiality should be discussed with the client. The rights of a patient in a family planning clinic should be carefully explained, particularly the right of the patient to choose her own method of contraception and her right to confidentiality. Most clinics follow a standard procedure, which is usually not questioned. It is up to the social worker to explore with the client exactly what type of followup she desires and to inform the client that if her wishes are to be respected, she must alert the clinic personnel to any reservations about followup procedures.

Direct Referral. Sometimes the social worker makes a direct referral to the family planning clinic because of a client's special problems. In such a situation, the following information should be stated clearly and briefly: client's full name, address, and phone number; nature of any special problems; what the worker wants the clinic or doctor to do; referring worker's name, agency, and telephone number. The client should be informed that a referral is being made on her behalf. The following case illustrates an instance in which direct referral by the worker is indicated.

When Mrs. T sought help from a family agency for marital problems, she confided that she had been keeping her use of contraception a secret from her husband. Mrs. T explained that her husband had always refused to use any form of birth control other than the rhythm method, as he believed that it would interfere with their sexual satisfaction. His strict Roman Catholic background prevented him from even considering contraceptive counseling to clarify this belief. Following the birth of the T's fifth child, marital conflicts increased. Mrs. T secretly received contraceptive care from a family planning clinic, although she too was Catholic. Now she was feeling extremely guilty because she had deceived her husband and had gone against the teachings of her religion. It was obvious to the worker that Mrs. T had a special problem requiring not only contraceptive counseling, but also religious counseling. Fortunately, the social worker knew that the family planning clinic had an excellent working relationship with several Catholic priests who were trained to handle such problems.

With Mrs. T's consent, the worker called a counselor at the family planning clinic and requested this combined service. Mrs. T was very receptive because she had received help at the family planning clinic before, but at that time had not discussed the religious problem. Mrs. T preferred postponing further counseling at the family agency until the other problems were resolved, and she was assured of the social worker's continued interest in helping her in the future.

If the client lives in a community where there is no family planning clinic, or if she prefers to go to a private physician, the worker can suggest the names of doctors who have positive attitudes toward birth control. Should the client be unable to make her own appointment and desire assistance, the worker can make a doctor's appointment for her, being sure to supply the doctor with the same referral information she would supply to a clinic.

The worker should check with the client shortly before her appointment date in case there are any problems with transportation, child care, or finances which might cause the client to miss her appointment. Some family planning clinics provide transportation or child care when it is necessary. When the clinic does not provide such services, the worker may offer help in solving any problems so that the client will not miss her appointment.

Followup

Followup is sometimes provided by family planning clinics. The referring social worker, however, should determine whether the clinic assumes this responsibility. If not, the social worker may follow through by making contact with the client or, with the client's permission, the clinic or private physician. The social worker should also determine whether the client has understood the advice and directions about the method of birth control she has selected, and she should be alert to any concerns on the client's part that have not been resolved. It is important that the social worker reassure the client of her continuing interest and availability should problems concerning contraceptive use occur in the future. A referral is successful only if the client is satisfied with the method chosen and continues to use contraception effectively, as long as the need exists. The social worker's continuing support is of great value in achieving this goal.

Special care must be used in making referrals for sexual therapy. In less than five years, by 1974, approximately

3,500–5,000 new "clinics" and treatment centers dealing with sex problems were opened in this country; William H. Masters estimates that only 50–100 of these are legitimate.[2] The rest offer "superficial sex education at best and dangerous quackery at worst."[3] At present, there is no licensing procedure for such clinics and no way to monitor their practices. The result is that such sex-therapy quacks compound the difficulties for legitimate therapists. The American Association of Sex Educators has established certification for sex educators and sex therapists, to protect the public from inadequately trained practitioners, as well as to establish criteria for these specializations. This organization offers workshops for professionals in sex education and sex therapy; credit for participation in the workshop can be applied to the requirements for certification.

It takes courage to seek help for sexual problems. A male or female client who is treated by an incompetent may either experience greater difficulties in later treatment or may never again seek help. Therefore, referrals should be made with caution. Family planning clinics often know of qualified therapists, as do local medical societies and social workers or psychologists who are working in family counseling settings.

One final point about referral techniques should be made. Those social workers who are able to establish good personal rapport with other professionals are generally the most successful in obtaining services from other agencies for their clients. They work at developing good relationships with workers in other agencies and learn enough about the regulations and operations of those agencies to be able to break through barriers which block many from access to the full range of services. Establishing this rapport takes time and effort, but will result in workers' obtaining adequate service for their clients, with a long-

2. William H. Masters, "Phony Sex Clinics—Medicine's Newest Nightmare," *Today's Health*, 22–26 (November, 1974).
3. Ibid.

range reduction in the amount of time spent in achieving successful results. To watch a skilled caseworker in the process of making a referral is indeed an educational experience. She acts simultaneously on a variety of levels—providing understanding and support to the client, imparting information about the service to which she is referring the client, dealing with personnel in the agency of referral, and coordinating all of these elements into a unified whole. As noted before, the technique of referral is vastly underrated, but it requires highly developed interpersonal skills and is essential to success in most practice arenas. Family planning and sexual counseling are ideal areas for making use of referral skills.

IV
ADULT
COUNSELING

8

Family Planning and Sexuality

The contributions of social workers to family planning counseling are relatively new. Three basic elements of the social work process are involved in such counseling, each employing different types of skills. The first element, information and education, is primarily rational and factual, and includes the debunking of myths and misunderstandings, as well as the communication of new information. The second element, the making of referrals, incorporates the social worker's knowledge of existing resources and services and her ability to motivate and help the client to use these avenues of assistance. The third element, individual or group counseling, requires specialized skills in understanding, communication, and rapport. The goal of such counseling is to use family planning as a vehicle for increasing the client's ability to achieve control within her total life situation. Such counseling is often necessary in order to relate conception control to the unique circumstances of the client's life situation. Although these three elements can be analytically separated, clearly they are closely interrelated. Most casework interventions employ all three skills—information giving, referral, and individual counseling. In each instance, what is needed is knowledge about available services, opportunities to use them, and individualized counseling to relate the use of family planning to the specific problem-solving process.

The knowledge base necessary to implement the information and education aspects of social work process and referral techniques are covered in the earlier chapters of this book. This chapter will focus on pertinent aspects of counseling which may be applied in the helping process as it relates to family planning.

Social workers have access to many secrets of their clients. The assurance of confidentiality facilitates the client's willingness to share very personal information. It is important that professional use of such confidential, intimate knowledge be directed toward increasing the client's freedom of choice in matters of fertility control, without imposing the biases and goals of the social worker. Any hint of coercion or insensitivity in pursuing sexual revelations should be avoided; this caution, however, should not preclude an openness and an overt willingness to enter into discussions of sexuality and conception control.

Contraceptive Counseling

Family planners are faced with a dilemma. They are aware that clinic patients are more likely to be satisfied if they move through the clinic quickly. Clinical physicians are busy and see a large number of patients; a single doctor may see as many as thirty patients in one clinic session. Other staff members are pressured to keep the patient flow moving, both because of the patient's desires to be seen without undue delay and because of the necessity of not keeping the doctor waiting.

As a result, patients generally do not receive adequate counseling. The usual pattern is that a nurse or an aide gives a brief description of a variety of contraceptive methods to a group of patients waiting to see the doctor, sometimes showing a film or using other visual aids. Each patient is then interviewed briefly and asked her choice of contraceptive method. Counseling is usually confined to information regarding the use of the chosen method. The patient is then seen by the physician and given the contraceptive equipment. She is once again seen briefly by an aide or a nurse, who checks to see that the patient understands how to use the prescribed contraceptive method.

For many women who visit family planning clinics to receive a method of contraception, this procedure is all that is necessary. For others who have special problems, fears, or ambivalences, further counseling is indicated. Such services should be available, and those helping professionals involved in family planning education should be sensitized to identify patients who need referral for special services.

The usual educational approach in a family planning clinic does not allow for the identification of personal problems, confusions, and fears which interfere with the successful use of contraceptives, and is almost devoid of any sexual counseling. The feelings of the patient are usually not dealt with, nor is an attempt made to examine those aspects of her life situation which might impinge upon her use of contraceptives. In short, such counseling bears little relationship to the kind of help which social workers offer as an integral part of their professional repertoire in other settings. This help should be given to those who need to deal with problems and feelings before they can comfortably use a method of contraception.

Social workers have, in addition, their own problems. There is a general lack of expertise regarding the technical aspects of contraceptives. Historically, clients have been treated by public welfare workers as though they should be sexually inactive. Public welfare policy and practice have indeed been in a double-bind, when eligibility is usually based on the absence of the father from the home. For years, investigators have conducted checks to see if recipients are involved with men, and many clients have lost eligibility over such infractions. Now, social workers in the Aid to Families with Dependent Children program (AFDC) are mandated by law to offer birth control services to all clients who might need and want them. There is some implication that clients feel compelled to accept them as a condition of continued eligibility.[1] The assumption that clients are not supposed to have sexual partners still lingers. Florence Haselkorn quotes a workshop participant as saying: "Public assistance workers cannot immediately stop looking for the 'man in the closet' and discuss family planning freely."[2] Fathers sometimes qualify for AFDC, and queries related to the man's attitudes are usually omitted, reflecting a continued practice of a double standard in sexual morality. The well-intentioned AFDC worker may not even be aware of her bias.

Public welfare workers must be sensitive to the need for family planning, but must be careful not to use this awareness to pressure or to threaten the eligibility of the client. Public welfare policy must be carefully monitored, however; there is undoubtedly the temptation for many public welfare workers to pursue an antinatalist policy in the interest of reducing welfare costs. Taking this temptation into account, some researchers, while recommending more public welfare initiative in providing family planning referrals, also recommend that any followup be carried out by the agency providing the contraceptive services rather than by the public welfare agency.[3]

1. Bernard Greenblatt, "Family Planning Goals and Social Work Roles," *Family Planning Perspectives*, 4:54–59 (January 1972).

2. Florence Haselkorn, "Value Issues for Social Work in Family Planning: An Introductory Note" in *Family Planning: Readings and Case Materials*, ed. Haselkorn (New York: Council on Social Work Education, 1971), p. 211.

3. Department of Health, Education, and Welfare, *Services to AFDC Families: First Annual Report on Services to Families Receiving Aid to Families with Dependent Children under Title IV of the Social Security Act* (Washington, D.C.: U.S. Government Printing Office, 47–951, 1970).

Obstacles to Successful Counseling

Barriers to the use of family planning services can be divided into three general categories: client-related; worker-agency related; and situation-structure related. Although not definitive, a brief description of some of these can sensitize the social worker to the major impediments which interfere with effective family planning counseling.[4]

Client-Related Barriers

Miss G was socialized from early childhood to believe that women were successful only if they were sexually desired by men, and that true femininity was demonstrated by the capacity to bear children. She had never felt successful as a woman, and had reinforced her feelings of femininity by proving that she was sexually desirable to men. Since early adolescence she had had romantic fantasies of being desired and cared for by "Mr. Right." Brief affairs were seen each time as the answers to her prayers. Even though she was knowledgeable about contraception, she neglected using it. Each time, she believed that marriage was imminent, but that pregnancy would insure it and bring her and her lover closer together. On an unconscious level, her continued need to prove her femininity resulted in conception. When she became pregnant, "Mr. Right" deserted. The conflicts she faced reflected an ambivalence about the whole experience. She had been sexually desired and she had proved her femi-

4. Although there is some overlap, this categorization of barriers is derived from the many discussions of obstacles to contraceptive utilization found in the literature. See Miriam Manisoff, *Family Planning Training for Social Services* (New York: Planned Parenthood Federation of America, 1970); *For Caseworkers: Experience in Counselling Birth Control* (Planned Parenthood of Colorado, 1967); Katherine Kendall, ed., *Population Dynamics and Family Planning: The New Responsibility for Social Work Education* (New York: Council on Social Work Education, 1971); Frederick S. Jaffe and Steven Polgar, "Family Planning and Public Policy: Is the 'Culture of Poverty' the New Cop-Out?" *Journal of Marriage and the Family*, 30:228–35 (May 1968); Greenblatt, "Family Planning Goals"; Gitta Meier, "Research and Action Programs on Human Fertility Control: A Review of the Literature," in *Family Planning: Rearings and Case Materials*, ed. Haselkorn, pp. 227–44.

ninity, but she had also been used and rejected. This client needed a great deal of support. An understanding counselor helped her develop a belief in herself. Her need for reinforcement through masculine attention will probably continue, but an accepting counselor helped a great deal through her acceptance of the client, along with a joint exploration of the alternative of abortion, and repeated education about contraception for future use. Some women with repeated illegitimate pregnancies are expressing a dual need to prove their sexual desirability and feminine role success in motherhood.

This case material illustrates only one aspect of the numerous client-related problems which interfere with the successful use of contraception. The problems most often encountered are delineated below.

Contraceptive-related problems include: a history of method-related side effects and complications; previous failures or discontinuation of use; ambivalence or fear of specific methods, including fear that the method will decrease sexual enjoyment; opposition from the sexual partner; and moral or religious objections to the use of contraceptives.

Emotional and intellectual problems and needs include: low intelligence, which precludes use of methods requiring consistency and foresight for success; a history of being exploited sexually; the need to have a child in order to gain status, feel more important, or have someone dependent upon her; hostility toward parents or parent surrogates; a history of hospitalization for mental illness; a desire to become pregnant or to impregnate a woman in hope that this will result in a marriage; and an attitude of hopelessness and anomie, with a general lack of aspirations.

Problems related to the lack of correct information include: a lack of knowledge of contraceptive methods; confusion regarding the correct use of contraceptive methods; misconceptions regarding the menstrual cycle and the fertile period; myths regarding the effects of various methods.

Problems related to lack of relevance of birth control to other life concerns include: lack of a current sexual partner, especially following a recent separation or death of a partner; overwhelming reality problems not being resolved, which make it difficult to give priority to the use of family planning services; a general history of lack of prenatal care or preventive care for children.

Worker-Agency Related Barriers

Janet, a seventeen-year-old and the oldest child of a large Catholic family, had dropped out of high school because she felt that she was a financial burden to her parents. She left home and found employment as a clerk in a department store. She had been dating a young man for some while and had strong sexual feeling for him. Because she was worried about getting pregnant and desired to have sexual relations with him, she sought contraceptive counseling from a family agency. The worker who interviewed her had had limited experience and training. When faced with Janet's request for assistance, she focused on her religious background, her youth, and her sexual inexperience. She felt that giving Janet contraceptive information would be interpreted as sanctioning her sexual behavior, and that she would thus be contributing to Janet's problems. She was also fearful that the agency would be critical of her if she gave any contraceptive advice, and believed that she should refer Janet to a priest or to a Catholic agency. Janet had already rejected seeking such help and had pointedly requested contraceptive information. By attempting to divert the expressed needs of the client, the worker was imposing her own and the agency's values on her, thereby negating the usefulness of her attempts to help the client. By meeting Janet's expressed need for contraceptive care and recognizing her request, the worker could have helped Janet work through whatever conflicts she had, and could then have focused on any other problems she might have had.

This situation is illustrative of some of the dilemmas faced by workers in agencies. The major problems are noted below.

Caseworker attitudinal problems include: personal attitudes and values which interfere with the counseling process; attitudes toward clients which assume that any discussion of sexuality or contraceptive use is outside the workers' realm of expertise, responsibility, or involvement; attitudes which assume that nonmarital sexual activity is an indication that the client is unfit or ineligible for services (a significant problem among public welfare workers); stereotyped reactions to the race, sex, or social class of clients; and moralistic judgments about sexual behaviors.

Communications problems include: language differences; sociocultural, religious, and racial differences between social workers and clients served; misconceptions and misunderstandings between social worker and client; assumptions about the client's level of understanding or sexual attitudes and behaviors.

Problems of agency policy include: restrictive policies which limit the type and amount of family planning counseling that workers are permitted to give; lack of specific agency policy and guidelines, making it difficult for workers to provide counseling and referral; lack of agency initiative in provision of training and incentives for workers to acquire skills in family planning counseling; hesitancy to take policy stances which might incur criticism from special interest groups; any policies which attempt to pressure clients to accept family planning services as a condition for receiving other types of assistance; or any agency policy which makes sexual activity a basis for curtailment of services or benefits.

Problems of agency resources include: lack of staff or time for adequate counseling and followup services; lack of liaison ties with family planning agencies; lack of availability of family planning services and specialized diagnostic treatment services (for example, infertility clinics); problems of access due to limited service hours or location of facilities.

Situational—Structural Barriers

Mrs. H was a young mother of four small children. She had been deserted by her husband, had applied for Aid to Families with Dependent Children (AFDC), and was currently on emergency assistance from a local welfare agency. During the second meeting with the agency worker, she requested contraceptive information and was told to seek help from the family planning clinic at the city hospital for the indigent. She lived on the outskirts of the city, had no money for transportation, and knew no one who could care for her children. Agency policy did not cover paying the expenses involved in following through on a referral. The counselor at the city hospital could not make a home visit. Because there were already more patients coming to the hospital for services than could be seen promptly, there was a policy restricting any outreach efforts. In addition, financial assistance for transportation could only be provided for city public transportation facilities.

Several contacts between the family planning counselor and the welfare worker failed to resolve the issue; neither agency could provide sufficient financial assistance and each believed that the responsibility to do so lay with the other agency.

Such barriers frequently interfere with the provision of services. Other structural-situational barriers are discussed below.

Problems of group pressures include: pressures on women to bear more children than they desire or than they feel that they can adequately support; negative group attitudes toward the use of contraceptives in general or toward specific contraceptive methods; and negative attitudes toward family planning programs. Suspicions that the family planning programs are aimed at limiting the number of births within particular ethnic groups are often cited as a barrier to the use of family planning services. Such genocidal fears and suspicions are often heard by family planners and caseworkers alike, but research evidence suggests that they are not highly important deterrents to those actually in need of family planning. William Darrity and his associates found that black males under thirty were the strongest proponents of the genocidal charge, while women were much less likely to hold such views.[5] Our own research has shown that a distinction is made between the actual services and the purveyors of these services. In the black community, there is acceptance of, and a desire for, family planning services; at the same time there is distrust of the motives of the officials and administrators who set policies and run programs.[6] There is documented evidence that medically indigent blacks avail themselves of family planning services to a greater extent than their white counterparts.[7] Thus, these suspicions of genocide do not seem to be highly relevant to women who are in need of family planning services, as long as the services are made available, with no coercion or pressure, to everyone who wishes to use them.

Women share the major family planning goal of healthy mothers and healthy babies. Society will no longer accept the fact that maternal and infant death rates are from two to four times higher for poor blacks than for others. While family planning will not solve these problems, it is clear that they cannot be solved without the availability of family planning services.[8]

5. William Darrity, C. B. Turner, and Jean Thiebaux, "An Exploratory Study on Barriers to Family Planning: Race Consciousness and Fears of Black Genocide as a Basis" (Paper presented at the Ninth Annual Meeting of the American Association of Planned Parenthood Physicians, Kansas City, Mo., April 1971).

6. W. Newton Long, Barbara R. Bradshaw, and M. Burge, "Black Attitudes Regarding Contraception, Abortion and Sterilization," in *Abortion Techniques and Services: Proceedings of the Conference,* ed. Sarah Lewitt (Amsterdam: Excerpta Medica, 1972), pp. 151–60.

7. "Black Fertility Drops When Services Offered," *Family Planning Digest,* 2:7.

8. Russell Richardson and Naomi Gray, "Community Organization: Strategies and Techniques for the Provision of Family Planning Services," in *Family Planning: The Role of Social Work,* ed. Haselkorn

Problems of access to family planning services include: transportation problems; child care problems; agency service hours; fees for services which are beyond the economic resources of the client; intake procedures which discourage client follow-through; long waiting periods before clients can be scheduled for appointments, which necessitate hours of waiting before being seen by a physician.

Reality problems of living which take priority over utilization of family planning services include: severe economic problems; housing problems; employment problems; and severe interpersonal problems, including male-female role segregation problems, and cultural values which associate masculinity or femininity with large numbers of children. It is important to deal with problems in order of priority to the client. Motivation to use contraceptive services often occurs only after the client realizes that the caseworker is helpful in resolving other problems which are of pressing concern.

It is important that the family planning counselor keep these factors in mind; they are some of the many impediments which interfere with the effective use of contraceptives. It is equally important that the counselor be aware of the wide variety of incentives which most women have to control their own reproductive careers; because these incentives are discussed in several other chapters, they will not be enumerated here. When family planning services are available, women use the services, maternal and infant deaths are reduced, and the birthrate declines.[9] The task of the social worker is not to promote family planning, but rather to offer access to these services as part of the more comprehensive helping process.

(Garden City, New York: Adelphi University Press, 1968), pp. 124–30.

9. "Readily Available Free Services Reduce Infant, Maternal Deaths, Cut Birthrate," *Family Planning Digest,* 2:10 (July 1973).

The Male Client in Family Planning Counseling

The concept that women should take the primary responsibility for control of their own reproductive careers has been a basic feminist theme for generations.[10] However, when men object to the use of contraceptives, it is clear that success rates are lower. Further, as we move toward a less sexist society, men are becoming more involved in birth control. A thorough understanding of the various types of contraceptives on the part of both partners can lead to a mutual decision which in turn can open channels of communication and strengthen relations. Workers in family planning clinics are becoming increasingly aware of their primary focus on women and are making strong outreach efforts to involve men in the family planning counseling process.[11]

Many of the suggestions for contraceptive counseling can be applied to both men and women. Imparting sound information, making sure that this information is understood, and dealing with any fears, hostilities, or hesitancies are all part of this counseling process. The major difference is that the male partner is less likely to seek help and may be more reticent in discussing his feelings, particularly with a female social worker. Group discussion methods have been found helpful in overcoming these barriers, as have counseling and discussion with male physicians.[12] Because only two methods of birth control are available to men at present (condoms and vasectomies), both should be thoroughly explained. In most situations, however, the counseling process should primarily emphasize the supportive role of the male partner in birth control and birth planning.

10. Margaret Sanger, *Women and New Race* (New York: New Freedom Press, 1921).
11. Rose Middleman, M.D., "Services for Males in a Family Planning Program," *American Journal of Public Health,* 62:1451–55 (November 1972).
12. Paul Rysen and William Spillane, "The Effect of Education and Significant Others upon the Contraceptive Behavior of Married Men, *Journal of Biosocial Science,* 6:305–14 (July 1974).

Men need to be recognized not only as equal partners in the sex life of the couple, but as partners in those aspects that involve contraception as well. An effort on the part of staff to include men in the counseling process from the beginning might actually save time later, as men will more readily involve themselves in the decision-making process to limit family size. Definite steps should be taken by the worker to consider the client as a person, not merely in terms of his or her needs.

Four Practice Techniques

These are exciting times in the development of practice techniques. Partly due to the vigor on the part of critics who charge that casework efforts have been shown to be ineffective, new approaches are being explored and evaluation methods are being refined.[13] Leaders in the field are calling for the helping professions to use practice techniques that are effective.[14] Family planning counseling, being a relatively new field for most social workers, affords an opportunity to apply a wide range of approaches, particularly those most consistent with the overall goal of helping clients achieve control over their life situation.

For purposes of discussion, one-to-one interventions are used here, although group work techniques are applicable in family planning settings and have been used.[15] Individual counseling has been identified as causing the greatest concern when discussing the role of social work in family planning. Frederick S. Jaffe

13. See for instance, Joel Fischer, "Is Casework Effective? A Review," *Social Work,* 18:5–20 (January 1973), and Scott Briar, "Effective Social Work Intervention in Direct Practice: Implications for Education," in *Facing the Challenge: Plenary Session Papers from the Nineteenth Annual Meetings* (New York, Council on Social Work Education, 1973); and William Reid and Laura Epstein, *Task-Centered Casework* (New York: Columbia University Press, 1972).
14. Briar, "Effective Social Work Intervention."
15. "Unwed Teen-Age Mothers Discuss Their Mothers' Attitudes Toward Contraception," in *Family Planning: Readings and Case Materials,* ed. Haselkorn, pp. 306–10.

quotes a social worker as saying that she "wouldn't dream of suggesting birth control to a client unless she had been in deep therapy at least two years."[16] And Bernard Greenblatt contends that many social workers have a propensity to exaggerate the number of clients needing intensive counseling.[17] For these reasons, four problem-solving casework strategies have been selected as illustrative of how individual practice approaches can be applied to family planning counseling. These strategies were developed for people in need of help regardless of gender. See table 2 opposite.

The four techniques selected include: Helen Harris Perlman's problem-solving process; William J. Reid and Laura Epstein's task-centered casework; Lydia Rapoport's crisis intervention; and an adaptation of Lawrence Weed's problem-oriented record system.[18]

Perlman's approach was selected because of its general sensitizing nature, wide applicability, and broad acceptance in all fields of social work; Reid and Epstein's model is an integration of a number of short-term intervention approaches and lends itself well to many types of helping situations; Rapoport's approach is suited to specific situations in which contraceptive counseling is needed in handling a particular problem; and the problem-oriented record system is especially useful in medical social work settings when interdisciplinary cooperation is called for and when explicit evaluations of outcomes are indicated. All have a problem-solving emphasis and have compara-

16. Frederick S. Jaffe, "Family Planning and Poverty," *Journal of Marriage and the Family*, 26:470 (November 1964).
17. Greenblatt, "Family Planning Goals," p. 57.
18. Helen Harris Perlman, *Social Casework: A Problem-Solving Process* (Chicago: The University of Chicago Press, 1957); Reid and Epstein, *Task-Centered Casework;* Lydia Rapoport, "Working with Families in Crises: An Exploration in Preventive Intervention," in *Crisis Intervention: Selected Readings*, ed. Howard J. Parad (New York: Family Service Association of America, 1965), pp. 129–39; and Lawrence Weed, *Medical Records, Medical Education and Patient Care* (Chicago: Year Book Medical Publishers, 1969).

TABLE 2 COMPONENTS OF FOUR SOCIAL WORK APPROACHES

Problem-Solving Process (Perlman)	Task-Oriented Casework (Reid and Epstein)	Crisis Intervention (Rapoport)	Problem-Oriented Record (Adapted from Weed)
The facts of the problem are ascertained and clarified.	A target problem of the client's own choosing is selected.	Problem identification is centered specifically around a crisis situation.	A data base is obtained.
The facts are thought through by facing feelings, focusing on specifics, and understanding the implications of the problem.	Tasks for the alleviation of the problem are jointly delineated.	Tasks are directed toward a cognitive mastery of the problems involved in the crisis.	A problem list is drawn up. A plan is developed for each problem consisting of three parts: further information needed; action to be taken; client education and/or counseling.
A choice or decision is made by the client after a joint examination of alternatives and consequences.	A time period for task accomplishment is agreed upon. Progress and direction in task accomplishment by the client is the focus of casework intervention.	Counseling is geared toward basic information and education. Interventions are aimed toward creating a bridge to community resources and overcoming communication failures.	Progress notes are kept for each contact which include: subjective evaluation (client's description of feelings); objective evaluation (changes in status, physical findings, and so forth) assessment by caseworker (worker's evaluation); plan (any immediate plan for problem alleviation). A discharge summary is entered when the problem is solved or the case is closed for any reason.

ble components. They can be used in part, in full, or in combination, depending upon specific situations, client needs, and agency settings.

The following case history excerpts illustrate how these approaches can work in family planning counseling. Specific approaches are mentioned in the illustrations which follow, but elements of each are found within all of them. The problem-solving process lends itself as a sensitizing mechanism to most counseling situations. The task-centered and the problem-oriented approaches focus on defining specific problems and delineating plans for resolving these problems. Crisis intervention is also task-oriented, with an emphasis on rational understanding, direction, and utilization of existing community resources.

Joan was a seventeen-year-old high school senior who agreed at her mother's insistence to talk to a social worker in a family agency. At home her withdrawn and secretive behavior was interspersed with outbursts of temper. Her parents were concerned because the family was close and Joan had previously been an outgoing, responsive member. Within the atmosphere of acceptance and confidentiality of the family agency, Joan revealed that she thought her depression and anxiety were probably caused by the oral contraceptives which her boyfriend has insisted that she use.

The social worker knew that depression could be caused by the pill. She also knew that there could be other causes, and encouraged Joan to talk about herself. Joan's boyfriend was a twenty-one-year-old policeman who usually worked graveyard shifts. He was insistent that Joan come to his apartment almost every afternoon after school. She cooked, washed, and cleaned for him, and she perceived him as very possessive and demanding. Her parents knew nothing about the relationship and Joan expressed her feelings of guilt about it.

Using the problem-solving process as a general orientation, the social worker explored Joan's feelings about her boyfriend and about hiding her activities from her parents. Two sessions were spent in analyzing these feelings and working on the specific incidents which had caused the greatest distress. When finally faced with the question of what she was getting out of the relationship, there was a long silence. Then Joan responded: "Nothing much." "What about sex?" was the next question; "Do you enjoy it?" Another long silence. Then: "I hate it. I don't feel anything."

The social worker was able to help Joan see that sex was not something owed to another person. The worker and Joan explored what Joan expected from the relationship with her boyfriend. In the process of doing so, she saw that she had the right to expect certain satisfactions, including sexual ones, and did not need to respond to pressures from either her parents or her contemporaries. With support from the worker, Joan terminated her relationship with her boyfriend. She decided to discontinue the use of oral contraceptives, but was made aware that foam and condoms were available and were relatively safe. The social worker also made sure that she understood the workings of the menstrual cycle.

Thus, Joan had made several crucial decisions in the problem-solving process: to terminate an exploitative relationship; to demand satisfactions for herself in future relationships; and to use contraceptives of her own choosing in the future.

Mr. and Mrs. A had three preschool-age children. Mr. A, a hard-working clerk, was having a difficult time providing for the family. He had repeatedly suggested to his wife that she seek contraceptive counseling, and had even volunteered to go with her. He had made many attempts to use condoms but his wife insisted that they irritated her internally, decreased her enjoyment of sex, and were repugnant to her. Mrs. A had mixed feelings about all forms of contraception; these ranged from the belief that they would injure her health to the fear that they would detract from her femininity and her husband would no longer find her sexually desireable as a result of the mechanical devices or the odors and "mess" connected with foams and jellies. She had not shared these concerns with her husband. She would agree to do as he asked, but always seemed to fail to follow through because of emergencies, such as the illness of one of the small children. In desperation, and yet hesitantly, Mr. A called the family planning clinic to ask whether they would counsel a man; he was relieved to learn that they would. He was further encouraged by the acceptance and understanding of the worker with whom he spoke and her offer to either call his wife or to visit their home. When Mr. A told his wife, she began to realize that his real concern was providing for his family; she broke down, cried, and told him her fears. He was thus able to reassure her, and she agreed to go with him for an appointment. The worker, alerted to Mrs. A's concerns as well as Mr. A's, was thus able to direct the counseling so as to alleviate Mrs. A's fears about herself. The couple continued in counseling, and subsequently decided on a system of contraception that considered the emotional and physical needs of each.

Mrs. T was a shy, nervous woman who had never lived above the poverty level. She had had eight pregnancies and had six living children, the youngest only six months old. Her husband did not live at home, but it was believed that she saw him from time to time. Her only official source of income was her AFDC stipend.

Mrs. T had received prenatal care from the municipal public hospital, and the children had been treated there. Her present AFDC worker had been assigned to her case for two months and done a good job of coordinating the benefits available through her department.

Mrs. T had never asked for birth control help, nor used it. She had missed her post-partum check-ups after the two most recent births—the only occasions when contraceptive care might have been routinely offered.

Mrs. T may have known that birth control existed, but, in her world, sex and contraceptives were not something that one discussed. They were intimate details of her life which, like the visits of her husband, were not mentioned to a welfare official who was in a position to cut off her income. She was not only embarrassed to mention that she needed contraceptive help, she was also afraid of the questions about her husband's employment, and how much he might have contributed to his family—in short, afraid of questions about why she needed to use contraceptives.

Using a task-centered approach, the AFDC worker worked with Mrs. T to help her with the problems which most concerned her. She helped Mrs. T secure an extra clothing allotment and arranged for her preschool-age children to enroll in a Head Start Program. The caseworker then asked Mrs. T if she was interested in using birth control in the future. Because Mrs. T had evidence that this caseworker was concerned for her welfare, her usual reticence was reduced; hesitantly, she confided that she was very much afraid of another pregnancy. The caseworker responded by supplying both information and support. She assured Mrs. T that her welfare payments would not be curtailed if she went to a family planning clinic, explained what to expect and described what methods were available. They agreed on a target problem—unplanned pregnancy—and on the major task —the prevention of another pregnancy. At Mrs. T's request, the caseworker made an appointment for her at a nearby health department clinic. Mrs. T expressed fear that she would be asked personal questions, but agreed to keep the appointment. She also accepted the tasks of arranging childcare and transportation for herself. She and her case-worker made an appointment for a home visit the day following her clinic visit.

The followup home interview revealed that Mrs. T had chosen an IUD as a method of contraception. She seemed relieved to be able to describe her clinic experience to the caseworker—including her embarrassment and her confusion about what "checking her strings" meant. The caseworker again supplied support, expressed her feeling that Mrs. T had made a major decision that would be beneficial to her family, and explained how IUDs worked, including how they should be checked. At the close of the interview, Mrs. T said: "Things would be different if I'd done this a long time ago."

When Betsy went to college she became involved with a young, unmarried philosophy professor. Before the end of the term she found that she was three weeks late for her usually regular menstrual period. When she disclosed this detail to her teacher, his only comment was "It was your decision as well as mine. Don't try telling me I have to pay —you should have known how to handle it."

She didn't go home for Christmas vacation. She convinced her parents that she needed to go to England for the vacation as part of her educational experience. They were generous and understanding. She spent the extra money they had supplied for sightseeing on an abortion. No one was available to help her live through the experience or examine her feelings.

Upon her return to college, the same instructor congratulated her on her decision and asked if she would like to spend the weekend with him. One hour later, she swallowed a large assortment of sleeping and pain pills which she had been accumulating for several months. A class-mate found her in a semicomatose state and called the college infirmary.

Many girls have been expelled for such actions. Fortunately, the college physician chose to refer Betsy to a local mental health center, where she was seen by a social worker twice. In the first interview, she described what had happened and emotionally relived her experiences. She was much calmer in the second session, said that she thought she had resolved her problems of involvement with the instructor and was anxious to get on with her college career. The worker explored her feelings about using contraceptives. Betsy requested information about the local Planned Parenthood clinic, which the worker supplied.

Having lived through the crisis and been able to express many of the attendant emotions, Betsy did not feel the need for continued therapy. She did, however, make a visit to the Planned Parenthood clinic, where she selected oral contraceptives as a method of birth control.

The hospital social worker was called in for consultation by the head nurse on the obstetrical ward. Miss L had just delivered an eight-pound, four-ounce girl by Caesarean section. She was presenting serious management problems because of her alternating hostility and withdrawal and by her refusal to cooperate with the staff. The social worker, after obtaining information from the hospital chart, visited Miss L.

Miss L had had four babies in four years and was seriously obese. Although Miss L had little to say at first, the social worker, by maintaining a focus on problems which might be troubling her, was able to get Miss L to discuss her worries about her small children who were being cared for by a neighbor. The first interview ended with Miss L accepting the social worker's suggestion that a visiting nurse look into the situation and report back. The following day, after receiving the nurse's report, Miss L and the worker agreed that a homemaker was needed, and arrangements were made. The worker then was able to get Miss L to discuss her feelings about the hospital. It became apparent that communication with the foreign-born resident was a major problem. Miss L had had trouble understanding what he was saying. She also felt that he and the nursing staff were hostile toward her. They had refused medication for pain, and she perceived this refusal as punitive. Acting in a liaison capacity, the worker interpreted Miss L's feelings to the resident and to the head nurse; they agreed to try to reassure Miss L of their concern for her welfare. As Miss L became notably more cooperative, the worker brought up the subject of family planning. In response to a question about when Miss L wanted to have another baby, she answered: "Never!" Further exploration revealed that Miss L had occasionally used foam and condoms, but had never tried contraception on a regular basis. The worker explained the various methods, and Miss L chose an IUD. The nursing staff saw that Miss L had a supply of foam and condoms when she left the hospital, and the social worker contacted her just prior to her six-week post-partum checkup. Miss L kept her post-partum appointment and accepted an IUD as a method of contraception.

In the course of providing help to Miss L, the social worker had entered the following problems on her hospital chart: needs help in getting adequate child care during hospitalization; has communication problems with ward staff; needs help in selecting a contraceptive method. She then specified the plan for each problem and entered progress notes in the SOAP (subjective, objective, assessment, and plan) format. Additionally, she maintained her own case record, including an expanded data base. The discharge summary followed the same general outline.

These case histories are adapted from actual cases to illustrate the various possibilities in combinations of approaches which can be used in contraceptive counseling. The same flexibility can be used in sexual counseling, but with some additional considerations.

Although it is the accepted practice of family planning counselors to approach the issue of contraception in the way outlined above, a question as to when the client wants to have another baby could convey a covert suggestion on the part of the counselor that the client is expected to want another child sometime in the future. This is especially true if the client's religious background encourages large families or discourages birth control. It is strongly suggested that such a question be rephrased so that there is no possibility of misinterpretation on the part of the client. It would be far more in line with the concepts of freedom of choice for the worker to begin contraceptive counseling with a more open-ended question such as: "What thought have you given to how many children you want or can afford?" or "What do you think about the possibility that you may become pregnant again in the future?" Such questions facilitate a more open discussion of the issue of contraception and reassure the client that the worker is accepting of all alternatives. Once the client has become involved in the dialogue and is reassured that the worker respects her feelings and conflicts, contraception can be thoroughly discussed if a need is indicated.

It should be emphasized that none of the decisions made in these case illustrations represent permanent contraceptive choices. Within a total life-span, most women will make a number of decisions about the use of contraceptives. Therefore, followup and sensitivity to changing life situations are essential in family planning counseling.

SEXUAL COUNSELING

Two paradoxes should be noted in any discussion of the social worker's role in sexual counseling as it relates to family planning. First, most of the literature and practice in the field of family planning ignores sexual needs, feelings, and problems. Contraceptive counseling in family planning clinics is concentrated on method technology, human physiology, and reproductive biology. The language tends to be scientifically neutral. Sexual feelings and behaviors, in all their intimacy and tangled motivations, are usually ignored. There is the tacit implication that contraceptive behavior can be separated from sexual behavior and the emotions which it evokes.

Social workers, as experts in human relations, can easily see the fallacy in the separation of reproductive control from sexual behavior. But, as Florence Haselkorn has noted, social workers have their own paradox to face: they understand a great deal more about psychosexual development and the unconscious manifestations of sexual needs than they do about overt sexual practices and feelings.[19]

The scanty evidence which exists indicates that few of the professionals most often approached by people with sexual problems—physicians, clergymen, psychologists, and social workers—are trained or even adequate as sex counselors. William H. Masters and Virginia E. Johnson contend that patients coming to the average doctor with a sexual problem have little chance of successful treatment, and they do not fare better with other experts. In *Human Sexual Inadequacy,* they report that 48 percent of their patients had experienced failure in previous therapy. With the advent of many poorly qualified treatment centers, the record of prior therapeutic failures has increased to 85 percent since 1973.[20] Other studies indicate that a

19. Haselkorn, "Value Issues for Social Work in Family Planning," pp. 209–15.
20. William H. Masters and Virginia E. Johnson, *Human Sexual Inadequacy* (Boston: Little, Brown & Co., 1970); and William H. Masters,

great deal of misinformation, uneasiness, and conservative attitudes are held by physicians. Among social workers, there is a lack of training in human sexuality and a general tendency to avoid dealing with sexual issues even in marital counseling. If sexual issues are raised by the client, they are usually handled by the social worker in an intellectual manner. Such an attitude fails to help the client, whose real problems usually involve thoughts and feelings about sex.

On the positive side, however, is the rapid change which is taking place as social work practitioners become more aware of the need to deal with sexual problems. They have been among the first to recognize the value of research in sexual behavior and responses. Many have sought treatment and specialized training for themselves. This receptiveness to new approaches and solutions has made it possible for a growing number of social workers to adapt some of the newer techniques into their own practices.

An increasing number of social workers belong to the National Council on Family Relations, the Sex Information and Education Council of the United States, and the American Association of Sex Educators and Counselors. Through such memberships, they not only increase their own knowledge base, but also are in a position to make a contribution to the understanding of other professionals.

The average social worker has not had access to specialized training. She must, therefore, recognize the limitations of her expertise while exploiting her special abilities. When a client wants help with a sexual problem, the social worker uses the same basic techniques she would use in counseling in any other area: establishing a comfortable, accepting atmosphere; communicating on a level that is meaningful to the client; and facilitating the expression of

"Phony Sex Clinics—Medicine's Newest Nightmare," *Today's Health* 22–26 (November, 1974).

feelings to maintain open avenues of communication.

The various technical approaches to be used will depend on the theoretical and methodological orientation of the individual practitioner. Some of the approaches are outlined in the discussion on family planning counseling. Generally, most sexual problems which relate to contraceptive use are best handled by using one of the short-term counseling approaches, such as task-centered casework. Evaluative research indicates that short-term therapy yields objectively more positive results than other treatment approaches.[21] Perhaps the most crucial issue is to ask enough of the right questions in a manner which will enable the client to make an informed decision on a course of action.

In order to accomplish this end, the nature and scope of the problem must be ascertained. Harvey Gochros delineates four major sources of sexual problems: (1) lack of adequate information; (2) lack of clear, explicit communication about sex between partners; (3) lack of consensus on sexual activities; and (4) lack of sexual functioning.[22] Examples of these four deficiencies are given on the following pages. Although they are often interrelated, the social worker should be able to separate these major problem areas in order to develop a treatment plan. The first three problems are related to any difficulties regarding contraceptive use.

Although social work skills can be readily transferred to different problem areas, for social workers interested in the area of sexual counseling, specialized training is highly recommended. Minimally, the worker needs to be able to recognize her own limitations and to know when and how to make appropriate referrals. When no adequate re-

21. American Medical Association Committee on Human Sexuality, *Human Sexuality* (Chicago: American Medical Association, 1972).

22. Harvey Gochros, "Educating Graduate Social Work Students to Deal with Sexual Problems," in *Human Sexuality and Social Work*, ed. Harvey Gochros and LeRoy Schultz (New York: Association Press, 1972), pp. 244-51

sources exist in the community for treating serious sexual problems, particularly those concerned with sexual dysfunctions, it is probably best to discuss the lack of resources with the client without attempting treatment.

Other research complements the Gochros analyses by specifying three basic questions which should be asked in evaluating any sexual problem:[23]

First, is the problem based on ignorance? When a problem is based on inadequate information, misinformation, cultural attitudes which are handicapping, or lack of understanding of the needs of the partner, information and brief counseling are often the only services required. Consider the following case:

A problem frequently encountered among clients is ignorance on the part of both partners regarding the female sexual organs involved in intercourse. Mrs. B is eighteen and has no idea about the structure of her external genitalia, much less her internal sexual organs. She accepted her parents' prohibition against touching or manipulating her genitalia (especially masturbation) and against premarital intercourse. The use of sanitary napkins during menstruation prevented the minor exploration that using tampons might have provided. She and her nineteen-year-old husband, married a year, had no premarital relations; he has initiated all sexual experiences, using condoms for contraception. Mr. B, like many men, is even less informed that his wife about the sexual organs of the female. Their sexual activities are limited to genital intercourse with no foreplay other than kissing and Mr. B's stroking Mrs. B's breasts. Both are affectionate, and although Mrs. B becomes sexually aroused prior to intercourse, she has never experienced orgasm, as intercourse usually follows the brief foreplay. She has sought help because someone told her condoms interfered with reaching orgasm and that some other form of contraception would help her. She has also read some articles in popular periodicals about orgasmic problems in women.

23. Fred Belliveau and Len Richter, *Understanding Human Sexual Inadequacy* (Boston: Little, Brown & Co., 1970).

After some discussion, it is apparent that both Mr. and Mrs. B need basic information about the genitalia and encouragement to explore through diverse foreplay. Such actions will further Mrs. B's knowledge of her own sexual feelings and capacity for arousal. Mr. B has accepted the counselor's suggestion that he accompany his wife to the second session, and both are receptive to basic sex education regarding physiology and sexual functioning.

Second, is the client's problem part of the relationship? If the problem is one of guilt, fear, or situational dilemmas, ideally both partners should be seen together. This step might involve Gochros' second and third points. The following case illustrates a lack of consensus on sexual activities:

Mrs. N returned to the hospital social worker who helped her with contraceptive counseling following the birth of her last child. She developed confidence and trust in the worker during the previous contacts and is now able to bring up a long-standing conflict she and her husband have had over his desire for what she refers to as "unnatural" sexual activities. After some vague references, the worker is able to determine that Mrs. N is attempting to discuss oral-genital sex. The worker gives encouragement and acceptance by responding to Mrs. N's vague references, comfortably and openly verbalizing what Mrs. N has been trying to discuss. This makes it possible for Mrs. N to express her confused and ambivalent feelings about oral-genital sex. In the process of counseling, a great many of Mrs. N's misconceptions are clarified and some of her rejection diminishes as she feels freer to verbalize her feelings. Mrs. N gradually begins to understand the basis of some of her feelings—negative attitudes about the sexual organs and the secretions of these organs. She is able to explain to her husband why she has been unable to participate in oral-genital sex. She later reports that her husband has shown more acceptance now that he understands her feelings and the basis of her rejection. She believes she will gradually be able to explore this area of sexual activity if she is not pushed by her husband and is allowed to work through her feelings with the worker.

Masters and Johnson assert that counseling with only one partner in a relationship may "actually destroy or negate therapeutic efforts."[24] The following case illustrates this danger and is an example of a relational problem as well as Gochros' fourth source of sexual problems: lack of adequate sexual functioning. In addition, it reflects some of the problems found in sexual counseling with men.

> An angry Mr. F arrived at the mental health clinic to confront the worker who had, during the past three months, been counseling his wife for marital problems, which have been partly reflected in Mr. F's lack of sexual functioning. From the beginning, Mr. F had refused to join his wife in the sessions. He accused the worker of increasing their problems: the worker gave him an opportunity to express his anger and resentment. He felt that his wife's coming for help reflected negatively on his masculinity and her belief in him. After ventilating his anger and finding an accepting person in the worker, he was able to admit his own fear of his spasmodic impotence. From the history he gave, the worker tentatively ascertained that his recent lack of sexual functioning expressed through secondary impotence was related to what he believed was his wife's divulging of their personal sexual activities to an outsider. When his feelings were understood, he became receptive to the worker's interpretation of the problem as being related to the marital relationship and the problems which he and his wife shared. Once he learned more about the service available to him and his wife as a couple, and realized that the blame was not directed at him, he agreed to come with his wife for joint sessions to explore their problems.

It should be noted that referral to a specialist in sexual counseling is indicated if the lack of sexual functioning

24. Masters and Johnson, *Human Sexual Inadequacy*.

involved in a relational problem is of a chronic or deep-seated nature.

Third, did the problem precede the present relationship? If the problem is long-standing, the client should probably be referred for specialized treatment.

Special Considerations in Sexual Counseling with Men

Seeking help in the area of sexual functioning is seen by many men as a reflection on their adequacy. Men frequently convince their wives to seek help only for the woman's part of their sexual problems. Some counselors are well aware that a husband's need for help is just as great, and often greater, than his wife's. To involve the husband, however, it is necessary that the counselor tactfully communicate that contraception and sexual counseling are aspects of the marital relationship which require the participation of both partners and that the man is an equal partner in the marriage. The husband may be told that seeking help on his own, initiating the contacts for the couple, or involving himself on an equal basis with his wife in the counseling process implies strength and self-confidence on his part. Sometimes it may be necessary to involve him by requesting his help in understanding the problem that brought his wife to the clinic or by explaining the importance of getting his opinion of the total situation.

Many of the problems described for female clients apply to males: ignorance, misinformation, a lack of confidence. Experienced sexual counselors know that most minor problems of sexual incompatibility are based on problems in the couple's relationship or that the real conflict usually originates in other areas of their life and spills over into the sexual area. Just helping the couple clarify their communication and recognize where the real conflict exists can do much to improve their relationship and thus improve, or even resolve, the sexual problem. However, when the husband has a long-standing sexual problem such as impotency or premature ejaculation, it is extremely important that the counselor clarify the need for specialized help and refer him and his wife to a qualified therapist. This same approach has already been emphasized in cases where the wife has a long-standing sexual problem.

As noted previously, most qualified sex therapists require that both partners involve themselves in the therapy because the relationship between the two partners is involved at some level. There are qualified specialized therapists, however, who treat only the individual with the problem. Therapists also recognize that each partner usually has some sexual problem, even when one of the partners is identified as the one with "the problem" because his or her symptoms are the most obvious. This information has been repeatedly emphasized in the literature on problems and treatment for sexual dysfunctioning.

Desensitization, Relabeling, and Resensitization

As these cases show, social workers will find that they are often asked to help clients with relationships involving sexual problems. Within reasonable limits, a great deal can be done to alleviate these problems. One specific technique used by sexual counselors is desensitization: The term, as used here, is not to be confused with the specific method used by those trained in behavior modification. This process can be adapted by caseworkers without specific training and is important in helping the client work through sexual anxieties. Essentially, this technique involves discussing sex in a matter-of-fact way, using appropriate terms for sexual behaviors, and encouraging the client to accept his or her own sexual feelings and behaviors as normal.

Mrs. R came to the family service agency because she was deeply concerned that she and her husband were growing further apart since their sexual life had ceased. They are both in their early thirties, have been married six years, and have three children. When she conceived her last child, she felt resentful and blamed her husband for the pregnancy. However, having received sound contraceptive counseling following this, she has been using oral contraceptives and feels fairly confident that she will be able to avoid any future unplanned pregnancy. The youngest child is now six months old.

Initially, Mrs. R found it extremely difficult to talk to the worker, but with acceptance and encouragement she was finally able to explain her problem. At first she thought her husband had become interested in another woman, but she no longer thought so. She wondered if she had lost all her sexual attractiveness. She had never been able to communicate her feelings or her emotional needs to her husband, especially those in the sexual areas. She was deeply hurt, felt rejected, and did not know how to tell her husband. From the information she gave, it appeared that this couple handled anger, resentment, and rejection by silence and withdrawal. Mrs. R admitted that for years this had been her pattern: that her husband at one time initiated efforts to communicate more openly with her, but had not done so since she became so upset over the last pregnancy and withdrew from him sexually. She had been waiting for him to approach her as he always had in the past. She had never been able to take the initiative, but was able to respond to his affection and sexual advances in the past.

After several counseling sessions with the worker, who was comfortable and at ease in discussing sex, Mrs. R found that she too could talk more freely. She had been given some help in how to approach her husband by discussing sex openly and by communicating her feelings and needs. After five sessions, Mrs. R found that she could open this area of communication with her husband, tell him of her use of counseling, and suggest that counseling for both would help other problem areas of communication as well as the sexual problem.

Compared to middle-class values, working-class and lower-class attitudes are very often inhibited and restricted. Any deviation from rather rigidly defined "straight" sex is regarded as abnormal. In addition, there is a general tendency to avoid discussion of sexual matters. Many working-class couples have never seen their spouses undressed, for instance, nor have they ever discussed sex with each other. When sexual problems arise, there is a great deal of embarrassment and reluctance to seek help.

By listening carefully to what the client says, the case-worker can often help the client realize that behaviors which are enjoyable are acceptable. Talking about sex in an open, understanding atmosphere often frees the client to accept herself and her own feelings. Mentioning that other people also have these anxieties reduces feelings of isolation and abnormality. Often, the very problems which have been most troublesome to the client can be identified as sources of strength by the caseworker through the process of *relabeling.* For instance, the woman who desires a long period of foreplay prior to the sex act can be helped to realize that this is a sound way of building a good relationship rather than an indication of frigidity. An understanding of sexual physiology and functioning is also important if the client is to work through her problems and accept her own sexuality. Frequently, it is the husband who needs help in understanding the importance of foreplay. Explanations can help the husband who may be feeling that he is a failure as a lover because his wife is non-orgasmic.

Desensitization can thus be adapted by the caseworker as a technique which enables the client to discuss feelings openly and to learn that she is not alone or abnormal in the way she feels or in the ways she expresses her sexuality. The acceptance which results increases understanding and enhances feelings of self-worth. The successful result may be referred to as a kind of *resensitization,* involving a positive awareness of one's sexuality and a development of the ability to accept and talk about sexuality in a more comfortable, healthy way.

A major goal of sexual counseling is to place sexual problems in a context of natural expression. In order to do so, several basic principles should be kept in mind:

Sexual behavior is more than a mechanical reaction. Counseling should deal with the emotional and situational components of sexual problems. Sexual problems in a relationship are the concern of both sexual partners. This fact does not preclude individual counseling when the sexual problems of one individual are based on ignorance or anxiety-producing reticence, or are recurrent in serial relations.

Throughout the counseling process, the client should be helped to understand emotional and environmental influences on sexual problems. The social worker should neither dismiss sexual problems nor go beyond the level of competence with which she feels comfortable. Both extremes of ignoring sexual problems and of attempting to solve problems without the necessary expertise can be damaging to clients.

Finally, it should be reemphasized that sexual counseling and contraceptive counseling are highly interrelated. As Gochros has noted, social workers often overlook the fact that lack of contraceptive knowledge can impede sexual satisfaction.[25] When carelessly applied, contraceptive practices can either cause sexual problems or can be used to avoid dealing with more basic ones. An obvious example is that of a wife who avoids sexual relations by using the excuse of fear of pregnancy. Her failure to use contraceptives can hide her underlying dislike of the sex act.

Certain contraceptive methods may be seen as interfering with sexual spontaneity and enjoyment. A knowledgeable counselor can point out ways in which the methods themselves, such as the application of foam or use of condoms, can be utilized as part of sexual foreplay. As with all other aspects of dealing with sexual problems, the emphasis should be on understanding the client's feelings and wishes and establishing open communication.

25. Harvey Gochros, "Treatment of Common Marital Sexual Problems," in *Human Sexuality and Social Work,* eds. Gochros and Schultz, pp. 126–37.

In conclusion, Masters and Johnson introduce a cautionary note which all those involved in sexual counseling should heed:

"When duly constituted authority is consulted in any matter of sexual dysfunction, be the patient man or woman, the supplicant is hanging on his every word. Extreme care must be taken to avoid untoward suggestion, chance remark or direct misstatement."[26]

Sexual counseling should be kept in proper perspective along with other aspects of helping clients. Its goal is to help people achieve healthier, more satisfying lives, within the framework of freedom of choice in responsible, meaningful relationships.

26. Masters and Johnson, *Human Sexual Inadequacy*, p. 191.

9

Conception, Infertility, and Genetic Counseling

How Conception Occurs

Pregnancy is the result of the successful synchronization of several reproductive processes.

The menstrual cycle is perhaps the most intricate and delicately balanced process of the reproductive mechanisms. The first day of menstrual bleeding is called the first day of the menstrual cycle. The menstrual cycle extends from this first day to the first day of bleeding of the subsequent period.

During menses, the inner lining of the uterus (endometrium) is shed, down to its basic muscular layer. This lining is discharged into the vagina. At the same time, hormonal signals to an ovary stimulate the growth of one (or, rarely, more than one) of the female sex cells (ova) contained in the ovary. As the ovum (egg) matures, it produces a hormone called estrogen. Estrogen stimulates regrowth of the endometrium and triggers the release of hormones from the pituitary gland, which further stimulate the maturing ovum, causing it to burst through the surface of the ovary. This process is called ovulation and occurs at about the middle of the menstrual cycle. The ovum is momentarily free in the pelvic cavity, but it is quickly picked up by tiny finger-like projections (fimbria) at the end of the fallopian tube. The ovum slowly moves down the tube toward the uterus and is prepared for fertilization by the tubal fluids. The cells (corpus luteum) in the space left behind in the ovary after ovulation undergo certain changes and secrete a second hormone called progesterone, which prepares the uterine lining for implantation of the fertilized egg.

If conception fails to occur, hormone levels decline, and the prepared uterine lining is discarded with the onset of another menstrual period.

Spermatogenesis and sperm transport begins with the preparation of the male sex cells (sperm) in the gonads. It is a continuous process, unlike the repetitive menstrual cycle in the female. The sperm travel through many feet of tightly coiled microscopic tubes and eventually into a main duct (vas deferens). The vas conducts the sperm to two sacs near the base of the penis called the seminal vesicles. From here, the sperm are ejaculated through the penis into the vagina during sexual intercourse.

Millions of individually swimming sperm cells are included in each ejaculation. Once they gain entrance into the vagina, they swim up through the cervix and uterus into the fallopian (uterine) tubes. In the fallopian tubes, the sperm are prepared by the tubal fluids for fertilization of the ovum.

Fertilization usually occurs in the outer portion of the fallopian tube when the prepared ovum and sperm meet. The sperm penetrates the ovum, adding its genetic material to that of the ovum, and the cellular division begins as the fertilized ovum proceeds down the tube. When sixty-four or more cells have been created, they form what is called a blastocyst. The cells of the blastocyst begin to

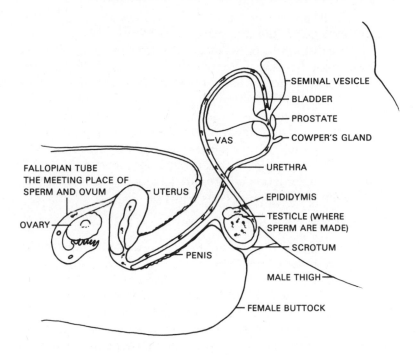

SEMINAL VESICLE
BLADDER
PROSTATE
COWPER'S GLAND
VAS
FALLOPIAN TUBE
THE MEETING PLACE OF
SPERM AND OVUM
UTERUS
URETHRA
OVARY
EPIDIDYMIS
TESTICLE (WHERE
SPERM ARE MADE)
PENIS
SCROTUM
MALE THIGH
FEMALE BUTTOCK

MALE AND FEMALE REPRODUCTIVE TRACTS DURING COITUS

differentiate into those cells which become the embryo and those which become the placenta (afterbirth), which supports the life and growth of the embryo.

Conception is the next phase in the reproductive process. When the blastocyst reaches the uterine cavity, and the endometrium has undergone further preparation by progesterone produced from the ovary, the blastocyst sticks to the prepared endometrium, immediately burrows into this tissue, and penetrates into the maternal blood vessels. Very soon after this, the conceptus (the whole product of conception throughout the entire period of gestation) begins to produce its own special hormone called Human Chorionic Gonadotrophin (HCG). At about six weeks after conception, there is enough HCG in the urine to give a positive pregnancy test.

The distinction between fertilization and conception is important because, scientifically, conception is the implantation of the fertilized ovum in the uterus. Those who object to the IUD or to the morning-after pill on the grounds that these methods of birth control cause abortion do not distinguish between fertilization and conception. They generally fail to realize that without any method of contraception, many fertilized ova do not implant in the uterus. Implantation failures are a frequent cause of infertility and early spontaneous abortion.

Infertility Counseling

Approximately 15 percent of all couples have infertility or subfertility problems which prevent them from having any children, or as many children as they desire.[1] In counseling clients who want children but have been unable to conceive, the following guidelines should be employed:

1. The social worker should make sure that both partners have a clear understanding of how conception occurs. This step requires some delicate questioning, not only about the level of knowledge of the reproductive process, but also about the sexual relationship of the couple. Do they understand that the woman is fertile for only a brief time during the menstrual cycle? Are they able to determine when this fertile period occurs, for example, by the temperature method? Is intercourse painful? (This problem may be associated with infection.) What are their attitudes toward intercourse? (There is evidence that psychological problems may cause obstruction in the fallopian tubes.) What is the frequency of intercourse? (Some authorities believe that both too frequent and too infrequent acts of coitus result in lowered fertility.) Often, conception occurs before any treatment begins. In one report, preg-

1. Robert W. Kistner, *Gynecology: Principles and Practice,* 2d ed. (Chicago: Year Book Medical Publishers, 1971), p. 458.

nancy occurred prior to any treatment in 122 out of 500 patients seeking infertility therapy—evidently the result of increased understanding or changes in sexual practices or attitudes.[2]

2. Couples, rather than individuals, should be seen for infertility counseling, diagnosis, and treatment. Infertility is almost as often a problem among men as it is among women. Because the male reproductive system is less complicated than that of the woman, it is less costly and more efficient to begin diagnostic work with the man. If male infertility is discovered, treatment can begin immediately. Causes of male infertility include: lack of a sufficient number of healthy, mature sperm (a normal ejaculate contains between 200 and 500 million sperm, and an ejaculate of less than 60 million is considered too low to result in conception[3]); obstruction of the tubes (vas deferens or epididymis) which conduct the seminal fluid and sperm from the testicles to the end of the penis; inadequate secretion of seminal fluid—the whitish fluid that carries the sperm into the female sex organs; and inability to achieve erection which results in ejaculation into the vagina. If no problem of male infertility exists, the woman should have an infertility workup.

Causes of infertility in the female include: inability of either ovary to produce mature eggs; an abnormal uterus, either in size or function, which does not allow implantation of the fertilized egg; and an unbalanced uterine environment which fails to nourish and protect the fetus.

There is evidence that 35 percent of all fertility problems are of multiple origin, so finding one cause does not rule out the possibility of others.[4] Regardless of the findings, both partners should be helped to realize that infertility is no one's fault; blaming an infertile mate can

2. Alan Guttmacher, *Birth Control and Love* (New York: Bantam Books, 1969), p. 207.
3. Kistner, *Gynecology*, p. 463.
4. Ibid., p. 460.

have no positive benefit, and may, in fact, hamper treatment.

3. Referral for infertility workups and treatment should be made early, as soon as any problem is recognized. Early diagnosis and treatment result in a higher rate of reversal of infertility. Infertility problems can be overcome in about 50 percent of the cases referred for infertility workups and counseling.[5] The basic rule is that a couple who have had normal unprotected intercourse for a year without conception should be referred for an infertility workup. If pregnancy has not resulted after eighteen months of unprotected intercourse, some undiscovered medical factor is almost certain to exist. The age of both partners is highly related to fertility; twenty-four is the optimal age for impregnation and conception. Fertility in women declines rapidly after the age of thirty. The frequency of intercourse is associated with fertility. The prognosis is poorer when male infertility is involved than when female infertility is a major factor.[6] Multiple causation frequently makes treatment difficult. The 50 percent success rate is expected to improve as new synthetic hormones receive increased attention and psychological factors are more clearly understood.[7]

Social workers should be prepared to help clients with infertility problems on two levels: by recognizing the symptoms of infertility problems and offering counseling and support to clients seeking help in bearing a child, including assistance in gaining the full cooperation of the male partner; and by referring the client to a specialist or infertility clinic with the necessary facilities for complete medical testing and treatment. Local resources can be found by contacting medical schools and teaching hospitals, Planned Parenthood affiliates, or other family-planning clinics. Many infertility specialists belong to the

5. Ibid., p. 459.
6. Ibid., pp. 464, 463.
7. Guttmacher, *Birth Control and Love,* p. 218.

American Society for the Study of Sterility. State and local chapters of the American Medical Association can furnish names of members belonging to this organization.

With the decrease in babies for adoption, resulting from the rapid rise in elective abortions, an increased emphasis on infertility treatment may be expected. Artificial insemination is an option of growing importance. Also, increased sex knowledge appears to cause a decline in infertility. Overall, infertility, as much as unwanted fertility, is an essential part of the major family-planning goal of, "Every Child A Wanted Child."

Genetic Counseling

Mr. and Mrs. C are carriers of sickle cell trait, but neither knew this until some of their children displayed symptoms which were diagnosed as sickle cell disease. They have eight children; four have sickle cell anemia, three have the trait, and only one is normal.

Gerrie, 16, is the oldest child. She has been in the hospital three times in the past year alone.

"A parent is under tremendous pressure not knowing when a child is going to have a crisis," says Mrs. C. "It's hard to explain what it does to you inside—any disease for which there is no cure. I remember going to the hospital to see Gerrie and she was in such pain she didn't even recognize me."[8]

Genetic counseling is a method of telling people whether they carry certain inheritable defects which, in the reproduction process, may result in still-born or damaged babies. Counseling about a genetically transmitted condition involves giving accurate information and dealing with the psychological responses basic to adjustment to the facts. It requires informed, specialized knowledge and is not for the amateur in counseling.

The primary purpose of genetic counseling is to answer

8. Shirley M. Linde, *Sickle Cell: A Complete Guide to Prevention and Treatment* (New York: Pavillion Publishing Co., 1972).

questions pertaining to probabilities, such as "What are my chances of being affected?" "What are the chances of my offspring being affected?" According to Dr. Richard M. Goodman, it is the role of the genetic counselor to present the facts in a clear and forthright manner so that the individual can judge for himself.[9] He suggests that a client be counseled about all the medical and emotional factors concerning a disease, in addition to the probability that the problem will occur.

It should be emphasized that genetic counseling may be, and often is, an involved and costly process. The most qualified individuals for genetic counseling are physicians who are trained in this area, geneticists who are personally motivated and interested in counseling, and social workers with special training in genetics.

It is traumatic for the individual to realize that he has transmittable genetic defects which can result in seriously damaged offspring, incapable of leading normal lives.

A serious concern in social work education should be to develop specialized training to supply a pool of qualified genetic counselors. Social workers have many qualifications which lend themselves to this subspecialization. Without a sound knowledge base in genetics, however, their expertise in the counseling process cannot be tapped for genetic counseling. With the developing technology for the detection of genetic defects, it is imperative that the social work profession keep pace in supplying qualified practitioners.

Above all, it should be emphasized that the better part of knowledge is an awareness of the limitations of that knowledge. A good social worker knows when the greatest help she can offer is to make a referral and give supportive therapy, without undertaking an in-depth counseling process; part of her expertise lies in having established her knowledge of the available resources which are appropri-

9. Richard M. Goodman, ed., *Genetic Disorders of Man* (Boston: Little, Brown & Company, 1970), p. 99.

ate to her clients' needs. Skilled social workers without specialized training can perform the vital brokerage function of referral when confronted with genetic problems.

At present, the contribution of genetic counseling to the improvement of mankind has been minimal, but the future is hopeful. Genetic counseling can, and should, play a vital role in decisions to have children, therapeutic abortions, sterilizations, adoptions, and marriage counseling. Conditions which call for genetic counseling include sickle cell anemia (trait or disease), diabetes, mental retardation, certain inherited kidney diseases, and hemophilia.

Although few physicians are trained in medical genetics, most university medical centers have such individuals. There are established genetics clinics at various medical institutions to which patients can be referred for diagnosis and counseling. Referral should always be made through a medical clinic or a private physician so that an accurate diagnosis of genetic disease can be made. Genetic evaluations are released only to qualified medical personnel for interpretation. Often, the clients will need supportive services from the social worker as they go through a variety of referral agencies.

All the genetic counseling units in the United States are listed in the *International Directory of Genetic Service,* published by the National Foundation for Genetic Services, 800 Second Avenue, New York, New York 10017.

10

Menopause, Sexual Activity, and Contraception

Approximately a month after their son's wedding, Mrs. B refused her husband at a specific sexual opportunity and, while doing so, told him for the first time that she had never had the slightest interest in sex, that she had fulfilled her wifely duties fully, and that it was undignified for a woman of her years to be expected to continue sexual connection. She insisted upon separate bedrooms.

If for no other reason than to prove once and for all the impossibility of authoritative contention that both pleasant and effective sexual function was possible, she reluctantly joined her husband in active therapy. Subsequent to elective reorientation of both husband and wife to the concerns of mutual communication and to detailed psychosexual education, Mrs. B became intrigued with the new information at her disposal, lost her high level of suspicion, grew totally cooperative, and soon became fully responsive sexually. She actually was orgasmic during the acute phase of the treatment.[1]

1. William H. Masters and Virginia E. Johnson, *Human Sexual Inadequacy* (Boston: Little, Brown & Co., 1970), pp. 345–46.

Menopause does not mean the end of sexual desires or responses or femininity. Nor does it necessarily mean becoming edgy or depressed. Changes that do occur during menopause, however, are real, and it is important that they be understood. An informed, alert social worker can help female clients avoid problems and seek treatment for symptoms which distress many women and their families. The following material describes the clinical aspects of menopause, with special emphasis on the uses of contraceptives during this period.

Menopause is the permanent cessation of ovarian functioning and menstruation due to physiological changes peculiar to human females. The average age for menopause is fifty, but it can occur between thirty-five and sixty, and may result from surgical or radiation treatment. The onset of menopause is caused by a reduction or cessation of ovarian production of estrogen, a hormone which is responsible for the development, growth, and maintenance of breast tissue and reproductive organs and tissues.[2]

Symptoms and Physical Changes

Due to a reduction in estrogen, a variety of symptoms may occur just before or during menopause. These vary from one woman to another, but the most common are hot flashes, sweating, and irritability. Less common symptoms are depression, crying spells, headaches, dizziness, and insomnia. Many women, however, never have any of these disturbances in connection with menopause.

Some women, even though they do not wish to have any more children, fear the end of their fertility. Others, view menopause as causing a loss of femininity and an end of their sexual activity. But for many women, cessation of menstruation and release from the fear of pregnancy are welcomed, and they experience an increased interest in sex.[3]

2. Herant Katchadourian and Donald Lunde, *Fundamentals of Human Sexuality* (New York: Holt, Rinehart and Winston, 1972), p. 91.
3. American Medical Association Committee on Human Sexuality, *Human Sexuality* (Chicago: American Medical Association, 1972), p. 80.

After a woman has undergone menopause, physical changes develop in the labia, the vagina, the uterus, and the breasts. Specifically, these changes are: a gradual atrophying of the breasts, ovaries, and uterus; a decline in the expansive ability of the vagina; shrinkage in the labia majora; a decrease in size of the vaginal opening; and, occasionally, a reduction in the size of the clitoris. Decrease in the production of estrogen also results in dryness in the vagina and thinning of the vaginal walls, which may make sexual intercourse painful if a water-soluble lubricant is not used. Usually, menopause with its attendant symptoms lasts for about two years, but the time-span may range from several months to years.[4]

In recent years, there has been a tendency among doctors to regard menopause as a deficiency state that should be treated. There is still medical debate over whether all women require replacement of estrogen, but there is general agreement that hormonal treatment should usually be given when a lack of estrogen has been established, as a cause of sexual dysfunction or other distressing symptoms.

Estrogen therapy is the prescription of synthetic hormones to replace what the ovaries are no longer producing. Many estrogen substances are now available in the form of tablets to be taken orally, and creams which can bring the lining of the vagina back to an earlier thickness.

Menopause and Sexuality

During the premenopausal phase, women frequently skip menstrual periods and fear pregnancy. In this phase, they also may occasionally ovulate even though they have not had a period for several months. The pregnancy risk to premenopausal women is, therefore, significant, and appropriate contraception should be used. Oral contraception may be very reassuring because it establishes regular menstrual bleeding. Many women in this age group, how-

4. *A Clinical Guide to the Menopause and the Postmenopause* (New York: Ayerst Laboratories, 1968).

ever, have varicose veins, high blood pressure, or other health problems which are contraindications to oral contraception, and other forms of contraception may be recommended.

Menopause does not mean the end of being a woman, or of sexual desire and response. William H. Masters and Virginia E. Johnson have pointed out that present knowledge of sexual problems of the aging is totally inadequate.[5] Social workers, faced with the task of counseling women

TABLE 3 SYMPTOMS OF MENOPAUSE

Premenopause	Menopause	Postmenopause
Irregular periods	The last period	No more periods
Hot flashes, sweating, palpitations	Hot flashes, sweating, palpitations	Occasional hot flashes
	Drying-out of vagina	Dry vagina
Crying spells		
Nervousness, excitability, irritability	Nervousness, depression	Depression
	Low back pain	Weaker bones, loss of height
Insomnia, headaches		
		Prolapsed uterus, vaginitis, sagging breasts, wrinkling skin
Fertility	Fertility	Fertility possible for one year

5. Masters and Johnson, *Human Sexual Inadequacy.*

with problems of sexual tensions during menopause or postmenopause, will find a shortage of literature on the subject. The first effort, however, should be toward relieving anxieties and fears. It is necessary to point out that, regardless of the changes in the reproductive organs, the aging female is fully capable of sexual enjoyment, particularly if she receives regular and effective sexual stimulation. Many women need to be reassured that an aging husband's continued interest in sexual activity is normal and may be gratifying. Sexual activity can continue as long as adequate health is maintained.

Male Climacteric

The term "male climacteric" is loosely, and sometimes inappropriately, applied to an array of psychological and sexual behavioral alterations occurring in men in the fifty- to seventy-year-old age group. There appear to be two components of the male climacteric that are discernible. The first is a relatively rare phenomenon occurring in men with various diseases which physiologically affects the testicles, such as mumps orchitis, with resultant atrophy; disturbances due to surgery, and genetically impaired testicular function, such as Klinefelter's Syndrome. With aging, these men do begin to have failure of testicular function with cessation of sperm and male hormone production. As in women, they may have physical symptoms such as flushes, increased irritability, lack of concentration, depression, and decrease in sexual drive and function. These symptoms can be relieved by the administration of male hormone replacement.[6]

In the vast majority of men exhibiting symptoms of "male climacteric," no such profound physical changes occur. Hormone replacement is usually not necessary or effective. There is no sudden drop in formation of sperm

6. Robert H. Williams, ed. *Textbook of Endocrinology*, (Philadelphia, Pa.: W.B. Saunders Co., 1974).

and male hormones in the testicles paralleling that of the female menopause. Instead, spermatogenesis continues along with retention of fertility. Testosterone levels remain the same or within normal range.[7] The condition is associated, however, with normal variations in sexual function resulting from the aging process; and these changes are likely to coincide with the changes in lifestyle, aspirations, and self-image that accompany menopause in women.

Masters and Johnson have established that there are certain subtle changes in male sexual function that occur with aging. They should not be construed as being incompatible with satisfactory sexual intercourse, "as long as there is an interested and interesting partner and reasonably good health."[8] Changes include, delay of erection in response to effective stimulation, prolongation of the plateau phase with a diminution of high levels of ejaculatory demand seen in younger men, and an increase in the resolution phase and refractory period. When coupled with environmental and lifestyle changes, these physical variations may be misinterpreted by the man and his partner. Because of social pressures ("too old for sex" and "the dirty old man" conditioning) couples may simply avoid sex. The male "fear of failure" complex may operate to produce a real sexual dysfunction.[9]

Counseling, and explanation of the meaning of the physiological changes occurring, may enable the couple to continue a long and satisfactory sexual relationship.[10] Occasionally, specialized sexual therapy may be necessary because of underlying, long-term psychosexual conflicts.

7. Ibid.
8. William H. Masters, Continuing Education Workshop on Human Sexual Function and Dysfunction, The Reproductive Biology Research Foundation, St. Louis, Missouri, July 16–27, 1973.
9. William H. Masters and Virginia Johnson, *Human Sexual Response* (Boston: Little, Brown & Co., 1966), pp. 248–70.
10. Masters and Johnson, *Human Sexual Inadequacy.*

11

Abortion and Sterilization Counseling

Abortion counseling is a new and challenging field.[1] Counselors will tend to be of greater help in this area if they believe in the woman's right to decide what she wants to do with her own body. Further, the counselor should be aware of her own attitudes toward abortion and

1. Techniques of abortion counseling are new, and most of what is written on the subject comes from women's groups which have been involved in this type of supportive role. In preparing this chapter, a number of such information and training guides were used including: *Abortion, Every Woman's Right: A Guidebook of Abortion Information* (New York: Eastern Women's Center, 1972); *Problem Pregnancy Training Manual* (Louisville, Ky.: Problem Pregnancy Counseling Group, 1972); Donna Cherniak and Allen Feingold, *Birth Control Handbook* (Montreal: Journal Offset, Inc., 1971); and Boston Women's Health Book Collective, *Our Bodies, Ourselves: A Book By and For Women* (New York: Simon & Schuster, Inc., 1973). More formal analyses include Christa Keller and Pamela Copeland, "Counseling the Abortion Patient Is More than Talk," *The American Journal of Nursing*, 72: 102 (January 1972); Miriam Manisoff, "Abortion," in *Family Planning: A Teaching Guide for Nurses* (New York: Planned Parenthood—World Population, 1969); and Leah Potts, "Counseling Women with Unwanted Pregnancies," in *Family Planning: Readings and Case Materials*, ed. Florence Haselkorn (New York: Council on Social Work Education, 1971), pp. 267-ND80.

pregnancy and should have dealt honestly with them. If such a person is not available to provide counseling, the next best person is one who can separate personal feelings from professional responsibility. Many people, experienced in providing abortion services, believe that women generally are more successful abortion counselors than men because they establish better rapport with the pregnant women.

Conditions and Methods for Abortion Counseling

It is important that counselors not be forced into abortion counseling against their moral beliefs. Any such coercion can have a negative effect on the client who is looking for sympathy and understanding but finds moralizing attitudes and hostility. A counselor who is sensitive to the emotions and fears which the client is experiencing finds satisfaction in abortion counseling because it renders an invaluable service at a time of crisis.

It is important too that an abortion counselor not be overloaded with clients. If this problem occurs, the client begins to suffer from an overworked, harassed counselor's trying to deal with too many people and problems, and a mechanized counseling situation develops. This situation contributes to the negative atmosphere of a "big-business abortion mill."

There is no reason why social workers who are interested in abortion counseling cannot add this skill to their traditional roles of helping women with problem pregnancies. A social worker should not promote abortion, but should include abortion as an alternative to a problem pregnancy.

As the social worker gains experience and confidence in herself, she will develop her own counseling technique as in other types of treatment. The social worker must feel and transmit respect for the woman and for whatever decision she makes. It is the responsibility of the social worker to help the woman's problem pregnancy become as positive an experience as possible, rather than a near disaster or a shameful, degrading experience. It is hoped that the woman will gain an inner strength, become aware of her feelings and emotions, and realize her power to choose and act on matters which involve her life.

Because the counseling sessions are relatively short-term, a counselor needs to have direct and specific objectives in dealing with a woman who has a problem pregnancy. Leah Potts has pinpointed these objectives:

(1) Provide information about alternative choices and resources. (2) Enable the client to reach her own decision concerning resolution of the unwanted pregnancy. (3) Help the client implement whatever decision she makes regarding the pregnancy. (4) Help the client, if possible, achieve some understanding of why an undesired conception was allowed to occur. (5) Plan with the client ways of avoiding future unwanted pregnancies.[2]

At the beginning of a counseling session, the counselor should help the client feel at ease. The counselor should introduce herself, tell the woman what the counseling session entails, and reassure the woman that confidentiality will be respected. The counselor should be alert to any fears which the woman might have which could cause problems in the counseling session. In order to establish rapport and to assess her information, a counselor may ask her client what information she has on the alternatives to a problem pregnancy. The counselor can then discuss any additional information which she has and offer to answer any questions.

The counselor should discuss all the alternatives to a problem pregnancy. Accurate, up-to-date information for each alternative should be provided. Alternatives to abortion include keeping the baby or giving the baby up for adoption. Emotional reactions vary with each woman de-

2. Potts, "Counseling Women with Unwanted Pregnancies," p. 270.

pending upon what she associates with each alternative. One woman may feel abortion is murder and cannot bring herself to have one, another may feel it is a greater sin to bring an unwanted child into the world.

Responsibility of Client and Worker

It is the client's responsibility to deal with her problem pregnancy. The counselor's responsibility is to help the client explore each feeling and emotion involved in the alternatives; she should never impose her own values and feelings. The counselor is important and valuable only because her responsibility is to her client—not to the boy-friend, husband, father, mother, or society.

If at any time a counselor begins to advocate a certain alternative, she is no longer serving the client's interest. Whatever the decision, the client will have to live with it for the rest of her life.

Whether a woman with a problem pregnancy decides to have an abortion or to keep her baby, or to give it up for adoption, it should be her decision and hers alone. While experiencing a problem pregnancy, many women realize more fully their own internal strength and their ability to decide on a course of action and implement it. The counselor's main obligation is to support the woman in whatever decision she chooses and to help her utilize the resources available to her.

If the woman should choose the alternative of abortion, the counselor should be prepared to give an accurate and detailed description of the type of abortion procedure the client will experience. Informing the woman of what is going to happen to her during the abortion will relieve many of her fears and anxieties related to the operation. The counselor should use her common sense and sensitivity, however, when describing the abortion procedure and not use language or mention details which will frighten the client or cause undue anxiety or worry. The counselor should be sure that the doctor and his staff are sympathetic and respectful.

It is important that the woman be encouraged to talk about her reactions to being pregnant and having an abortion and how she believes she will feel about it a week from now, and also ten years from now. This plan gives the client time to explore and talk about her feelings before the abortion. It is also a good time to talk about whether the woman wants to use birth control after the abortion and to explain the different contraceptive methods.

Post-abortion Counseling

Counseling before the abortion about what to expect after the abortion is essential. The woman should be told what she can and cannot do, no douching or tub bathing, for example, what the symptoms are if there is infection, perforation, or hemorrhaging[3], and when to expect her next menstrual period. The woman should also be warned that she might experience depression or sadness for a while after the abortion. This reaction is frequent and she should not be too upset by it. Although not experienced by all women, depression is probably caused largely by the hormonal changes in the body after having an abortion. The counselor should not act as if the hormonal reaction is inevitable, but the woman should be warned that she may experience it, and should be encouraged to call and talk to the counselor about it, if she wishes.

Once a woman has received an abortion, every effort should be made to followup. The counselor can set up a post-abortion conference, make contact with the woman by telephone, or have the woman return a post-abortion questionnaire. The information the counselor should check on includes: the client's treatment by the hospital or clinic, doctors, nurses, and counselors; whether the woman is using any birth control; and how the woman reacted emotionally to the abortion.

3. See, The Boston Women's Health Collective, *Our Bodies, Ourselves: A Book By and For Women,* p. 147.

A small percentage of women seem to have problems in their adjustment after an abortion. The counselor should either set up another appointment for a counseling session or should refer the client for longer treatment with a sympathetic helping professional. With experience, the counselor will learn to recognize in advance the women who will feel guilty or have emotional problems after an abortion and can try to guide them toward another alternative before the abortion takes place.

Counseling for Sterilization

The following examples are representative of the issues and questions which arise when counseling clients who seek voluntary sterilization. Ideally, the counselor should make sure that neither party is being pressured into consent. In actual practice, the counselor may be put into the position of having to choose whether to support the desire for sterilization on the part of the woman when the man is reluctant to give consent. Particularly with women who have had a number of children or who have health problems, such support may be necessary for the overall well-being of the family.

The counselor should be aware of the rules and regulations of local clinics and hospitals regarding sterilization procedures. Despite fairly liberal laws regarding voluntary sterilization, many hospitals have had restrictive policies. For instance, the Rule of 120 is sometimes used to decide who may receive sterilization. By this rule, the only people eligible for a voluntary sterilization are those whose age multiplied by their number of pregnancies is equal to or great than 120.[4] Although the worker may choose to work to change regulations, knowledge of policies is necessary if she is to make successful referrals.

The counselor should ensure that the client understands the surgical procedure and that it is intended to be

4. Helen Edey, "Sterilization," in *Foolproof Birth Control*, ed. Lawrence Lader (Boston: Beacon Press, 1972), p. 44.

permanent. If the tube or vas is properly interrupted surgically, it does not "grow together" spontaneously. Many clients have questions which they are reluctant to ask; a clear explanation, even unsolicited, can relieve anxiety and doubt.

A patient undergoing any surgical procedure, including sterilization, must be legally capable of giving informed consent; that is, he must be legally of age and mentally competent. If sterilization is considered without informed consent, clear legal permission, probably a court order, must be obtained. Special legal questions regarding sterilization can be answered by contacting the Association for Voluntary Sterilization, 708 Third Avenue, New York, New York 10017, or any of their branch offices.

Many men and women fear that sterilization will harm their sexual activities. Many women do not realize they will still menstruate after tubal ligation. Reassurances should be part of the explanation process. Many women believe that tubal ligations can only be performed following a delivery. It should be explained that pregnancy is not necessary for a tubal ligation.

Recovery time and process is another area of great concern. What to expect should be clearly discussed. Women with child care arrangements to make should be counseled to arrange for some extra help in case of unforeseen problems.

If sterilization is desired, but cannot be scheduled right away, some other method of contraception should be offered. Depo Provera is frequently given to women awaiting sterilization.

V

Adolescent Counseling

12

Adolescent Sexuality

I think [love is] giving yourself to somebody—really giving—and caring for that person more than yourself. It's a kind of a loss of all self-concern at one point. It's like I feel I have to give myself in all ways, and you don't become attached at all to what you might feel. You just give whatever you can to them—you think of them before anything else—before yourself. . . . At first when you get it you become a little frightened, because you don't know how far you're getting into it.[1]

Although adults have long been concerned about adolescent sexuality, their own anxieties about sex and their difficulties in communicating with young people have thwarted research into adolescent sexuality. Robert Sorenson's Report, *Adolescent Sexuality in Contemporary America. Personal Values and Sexual Behavior. Ages 13–19* is a survey researcher's approach to the study of adolescent sexuality. As of 1973, it was the

1. Robert C. Sorenson, *Adolescent Sexuality in Contemporary America. Personal Values and Sexual Behavior.* Ages 13–19 (New York: World Publishing Company, 1973), p. 233.

most ambitious survey of the sexual values and behavior of this population.[2]

Although sex is important, even in infancy, it is during adolescence that the sex drive becomes stronger and more conscious. The mystery of sex and the many ways it can be expressed offer the adolescent new opportunities for feeling and experiencing.

Sexual Intercourse

How prevalent is intercourse among adolescents, and what are their attitudes toward it? In Sorensen's group of thirteen- to nineteen-year-olds, 48 percent were virgins and 52 percent had had sexual intercourse at least once (59 percent of the boys and 45 percent of the girls).[3] Seventeen percent of all adolescents described as sexual beginners had engaged in sexual foreplay and 22 percent had had no sexual experience beyond kissing.[4] These sexual beginners described their families as stable and happy and reported parental guidance and discussions about sex more often than did the sexually experienced groups.

The first intercourse for 40 percent of nonvirgin adolescents in Sorensen's study took place in their own or their partners' homes. Girls most frequently reported fear after their first intercourse, whereas boys reported excitement as their immediate reaction. In general, a much higher percentage of boys than girls felt positive about their first experience of intercourse. Despite their more negative feelings, however, girls were more likely than boys to consider the relationship with their sexual partner strengthened as a result of this first intercourse (56 percent of the girls and 41 percent of the boys).[5]

Plans and obligations for marriage were not primary prerequisites for intercourse, but respondents viewed commitment to another person as basic to good sexual

2. Ibid., pp. 121, 122.
3. Ibid., p. 111.
4. Ibid., p. 149, 171.
5. Ibid., p. 214.

relations. The two kinds of love most frequently described were "durable love," which involves a strong commitment and a plan to marry, and "transient love," which is short-term, although perhaps intense.[6] The majority of adolescents interviewed believed that honesty between sexual partners, mutuality in deriving sexual satisfaction, and an emphasis on the quality of a relationship were more important prerequisites to sexual intercourse than was the duration of the relationship.

Serial monogamy with no assumption of marriage is becoming increasingly prevalent. Nearly half of the monogamists in Sorensen's group had had sex with only one partner, and most of these relationships had lasted for a year or more.[7] Eighty-eight percent of all monogamists reported considerable satisfaction with their sex lives.[8] They did, in fact, appear to be a responsible and healthy group. Of all the sexually active adolescents, the monogamists had used contraceptives most frequently and consistently, and female monogamists reported experiencing orgasm more often than nonmonogamists in the study.[9]

Nonmonogamous sexual adventuring describes the sexual behavior pattern of 15 percent of the adolescents studied by Sorensen (24 percent of all boys and 6 percent of all girls).[10] In sexual adventuring, the relationship itself is secondary to the desire for freedom to have sex with anyone. Most sexual adventurers felt that sex was a good way for two people to become acquainted, and they emphasized the physical benefits derived from sex as an activity. The sexual adventurers were more technique-oriented and less likely to relate to their partners in nonsexual matters. Females in this group reported having orgasm much less frequently than girls in the monogamy group.[11]

6. Ibid., pp. 111–113, 117.
7. Ibid, pp. 220, 245.
8. Ibid, p. 240.
9. Ibid., pp. 226, 245.
10. Ibid., p. 249.
11. Ibid., pp. 280–282.

Pregnancy

Conception occurred at least once to 23 percent of all nonvirgin adolescent females in Sorensen's study.[12] Although half of the sexually active females reported that they feared pregnancy enough to have avoided intercourse sometimes, the most sexually active were the most likely to use a method of contraception. The birth control methods reported by girls were oral contraceptives (33 percent), withdrawal (17 percent), condoms (9 percent), and intrauterine devices (2 percent).[13] The Sorensen study found that many adolescents had used no method of contraception the last time they had had intercourse, and that the majority had not been told about birth control by their parents (68 percent of all girls and 80 percent of all boys).[14]

Sexually active adolescent females reported the following primary reasons for their failure to use birth control devices: 98 percent of the girls who did not take any precautions against pregnancy reported that they did not know where to get a reliable contraceptive; almost 75 percent of the females rejected planning ahead for sexual intercourse; approximately 50 percent of the females interviewed did not use contraception of any kind because of a fear that parents would find their contraceptives; a lack of motivation was verbalized by 40 percent of the nonvirgin females, "Sometimes I really don't care whether or not I become pregnant."[15]

Most respondents (especially the sexual adventurers) were not opposed to abortions for others, but most sexually active females stated a preference for bearing and rearing their own children. Not surprisingly, sexually inexperienced teen-agers were less supportive of both abortion and out-of-wedlock childbirth.[16]

12. Ibid., p. 324.
13. Ibid., pp. 316, 325–326.
14. Ibid., pp. 318–326.
15. Ibid., pp. 322–326.
16. Ibid., p. 325.

TABLE 4   REASON FOR NOT USING CONTRACEPTIVES
(GIRLS)*

	All	Ages 13–15	Ages 16–19
Lack of information from parents	68%	69%	68%
Lack of availability			
Nowhere to obtain contraceptives	30%	46%	18%
Cannot afford contraceptives	17%	25%	13%
Opposition in principle or religious objection	13%	17%	10%
Lack of motivation			
Personal carelessness	45%	—	—
Too much trouble (except pill)	45%	35%	49%
Concern that parents will find birth control device	29%	58%	17%
Disapproval by sex partner	8%	15%	6%
Belief that spontaneity of sex act is hurt	67%	64%	68%
Belief that birth control is boy's responsibility	14%	20%	9%
Abortion is alternative	14%	21%	11%
Belief that pregnancy is impossible	30%	39%	22%

*These percentages reflect both reasons for never using contraceptives and reasons for not using specific contraceptives even when some form of birth control is practiced. From the presented data, it is not possible to distinguish between contraceptive users and nonusers.

Note: This table is derived from Robert Sorensen, *Adolescent Sexuality in Contemporary America. Personal Values and Sexual Behavior. Ages 13–19* (New York: World Publishing Co., 1973), pp. 318–327.

Venereal Disease

The spread of venereal disease has reached almost epidemic proportions in the United States, and many young people are aware of its seriousness. However, most adolescents interviewed by Sorensen did not believe that they would have sexual intercourse with anyone infected with a veneral disease. Even when they were willing to confront the reality that among nonvirgin adolescents the prevalence of veneral disease is about the same as that of pregnancy, (11 percent), they were reluctant to seek information, especially from their parents.[17]

Most adolescents felt that their parents were not willing to recognize their own sexual problems and behaviors let alone those of their children. Consequently, in regard to sexual behavior, 55 percent of the boys and 48 percent of the girls told their parents only what they believed the adults would consider acceptable. Many of the sexually inexperienced adolescents believed that their parents assumed that they had had sexual intercourse, and some felt pressured into early sexual activities by their parents' concern.[18]

Masturbation

Once defined as deviant behavior, manipulating one's own genitals to induce sexual pleasure is now regarded by many persons as a healthy activity. Nevertheless, young people were more reluctant to talk about masturbation than any other sexual practice. The Sorensen research yielded the following information: 49 percent of all adolescents reported having masturbated, although Sorensen believes this practice to be underreported. He also determined that females masturbate at an earlier age (before eleven) than males (before or at thirteen). Adolescents do not, as a rule, believe the old superstitions about masturbation affecting potency or sexual and personal adjustment, but they do express some personal distaste about handling their own bodies to relieve sexual tension.[19]

Homosexuality

The practice of homosexuality is becoming increasingly visible, but it appears to be mainly an adult phenomenon. Sorensen's research revealed little homosexual behavior

17. Ibid., pp. 331–338.
18. Ibid., pp. 79, 83–84.
19. Ibid., pp. 143–144.

among adolescents; only 9 percent reported having had any homosexual experience. In addition, the common view that children are seduced by adults is not substantiated; the majority of respondents reported having had their first homosexual experience with someone their own age or younger.[20]

Adolescents are tolerant of homosexuality for others and use the label *homosexual* to denote the act rather than individuals. Adolescents would like to see changes in our society's practice of labeling as homosexual even slight variations from stereotypic male or female behavior. They are more concerned about laws against rape (which they support) than laws against homosexuality (which they do not support).[21]

TABLE 5 APPROVAL OF SEXUAL INTERCOURSE BEFORE MARRIAGE

	Agree	Disagree	Not Sure
All Adolescents	76%	23%	1%
Boys	80%	18%	2%
Boys 13–15	70%	29%	1%
Boys 16–19	88%	9%	3%
Girls	72%	28%	0
Girls 13–15	65%	35%	0
Girls 16–19	77%	23%	0
Virgins	58%	40%	2%
Inexperienced	44%	55%	1%
Beginners	77%	20%	3%
Nonvirgins	92%	7%	1%
Monogamists	97%	3%	0
Adventurers	92%	6%	2%

NOTE: This table is derived from Robert Sorensen, *Adolescent Sexuality in Contemporary America. Personal Values and Sexual Behavior. Ages 13–19* (New York: World Publishing Co., 1973), p. 410.

20. Ibid., pp. 285, 294.
21. Ibid., pp. 294–295.

Marriage

An obligation to marry is not a consideration of adolescents when they are fulfilling their sexual needs. They do not feel pressured to legalize a sexual relationship. The old religious and moral teachings of a generation ago are no longer operative among almost 75 percent of the adolescents studied.[22]

In addition to challenging the sexual codes of their parents' generation, young people are also challenging the institution of marriage. They view the traditionally stereotyped male and female roles as discouraging love and intimacy. Sorensen suggests that if many young people continue to live together, marriage will occur on a more discriminating basis, later in life, rather than from pressure to satisfy sexual desire. Perhaps the divorce rate will then decrease as today's adolescents' serial monogamy without marriage replaces the legal serial monogamy of their parents' generation.

How Much Has Changed?

The ways in which the sexual practices of today's adolescents differ from those of past generations are much debated; evidence suggests that today's increased illegitimacy rate may be explained largely by physiological and medical changes rather than by increased adolescent sexual activity. According to a study by Phillips Cutright, improved health conditions and better nutrition have resulted in a lower age of menstrual onset; a possible decrease in the length of the sterile period following the beginning of menstruation; and an increase in the likelihood that an out-of-wedlock conception will be carried to term. In 1870, the average of menstrual onset was 16.5 years; in the 1930s it was 14.5 years; by 1950, it was 13.5 years; and by the late 1960s it was down to 12.5 years. Between 1940 and 1960, fetal loss to adolescents declined

22. Ibid., p. 341.

by some 20 percent. By combining an earlier age of fertility with a decreased likelihood of spontaneous abortions, increased sexual activity among adolescents accounts for only 11.5 percent of the out-of-wedlock conceptions which result in marriage and for less than 1 percent of the illegitimate births. Thus, the so-called sexual revolution may be, in part, a health revolution.[23]

Unfortunately, our society maintains a tradition of restrictive laws and customs which inhibit the development of realistic programs to deal with teen-age sexuality. Marjorie A. Costa, director of the former National Center for Family Planning Services, has recommended giving sexually active teen-agers high priority in the delivery of family planning services.[24] Throughout the country, there are ever-increasing efforts to gear programs to the needs of today's adolescents.[25]

Social Class Differences

This subject was not covered by Sorensen's interviewing and apparently he found no important distinctions. Other researchers, however, have noted some behaviors that are important in counseling lower-income teen-agers.

As is true for all sexually active adolescents, serial monogamy is the prevalent pattern among sexually active, lower-class youth, both black and white.[26] Illegitimacy rates are higher among lower-class teen-agers, especially among blacks.[27] There is also a greater likelihood that black girls will keep their babies rather than relinquish them for placement—a likelihood that is related to the

23. Phillips Cutright, "The Teen-age Sexual Revolution and the Myth of the Abstinent Past," *Family Planning Perspectives*, 4:24–31 (January 1972).

24. Marjorie A. Costa as quoted in *Family Planning Digest*, 2:3–4 (May 1973).

25. Theodore Irwin, "Birth Control for Teen-agers," *Sexual Behavior*, February 1972, pp. 41–46.

26. Sadja Goldsmith et al., "Teen-agers, Sex and Contraception," *Family Planning Perspectives*, 4:32–38 (January 1972).

27. Cutright, "The Teen-age Sexual Revolution," p. 25.

well-known fact that there is a scarcity of adoptive and foster homes for black children for reasons given below. There is no clear indication that premarital intercourse is more frequent among economically deprived black adolescents, however, but simply that their options are more limited. At least until recently, abortions were a luxury only the more affluent could afford. Stable, long-term relationships are frequent between lower-class teenage parents, even when marriage does not occur. The unwed father often shows great concern and responsibility toward his child. All too often, his existence is ignored by social workers and other professionals involved in helping the unwed mother.[28]

Middle-class blacks have a smaller desired and actual family size than any other group in the United States. As social workers who have worked in child placement can attest, affluent blacks are usually reluctant to adopt non-related children. Thus, there is almost no adoption market for black babies—about 99 percent of all such adoptions are by white families.[29]

Sex is often used as a trade-off by economically deprived girls for gains in security and status. Because sex is one of the few "assets" held by the lower-class girl, it is potentially more highly prized by her and may be used more judiciously than by girls with greater resources.[30] Precisely because they do have few other resources, lower-class girls have less to offer and therefore must use sex as a bargaining wedge more often, and are more likely to be exploited sexually. Thus, the use of sex is often a balance for the lower-class girl between what she stands to gain from its use and what she may lose through its misuse.

28. Phyllis Ewer and James Gibbs, Relationships with the Putative Father and the Use of Contraception in a Population of Black, Ghetto, Adolescent Mothers (Chicago: Department of Sociology, University of Illinois, (January 1973).

29. Phyllis Ewer, Atlanta Adolescent Pregnancy Project Evaluation Unit, personal communication, 1971.

30. Clark Vincent, Unmarried Mothers (Glencoe, Ill.: The Free Press, 1963).

The use of contraceptives can be vital in helping economically deprived girls gain satisfaction, status, and security. Sexually active, lower-class girls who use oral contraceptives correctly have significantly higher mobility aspirations than those who do not. They report enjoying sex and caring about their sexual partners, and they do not appear to be sexually exploited.[31]

In contrast to their parents' generation, adolescents are not depersonalizing sex. Probably, Sorensen's most important finding is that teen-agers are regarding sexuality as a natural phenomenon. Most adolescents value love and affectionate relations, and treat each other more as whole persons than as sexual objects. Adolescents are asking about the purposes served by sex. Unfortunately, they are not getting the answers they seek and need about sexuality and contraception and have often not found the available sources helpful or informative.

31. William L. Graves and Barbara R. Bradshaw, "What Are Your Plans for the Next Baby? Contraceptive Use and Early Reconception Among Black Teenagers after an Illegitimate Birth," in *Advances in Planned Parenthood* (Amsterdam: Excerpta Medica, 1974).

13

Counseling
Adolescents

You pick out your own ideas after listening to your parents. I
have to decide on the basis of my own experience. Basically, I
wish they would let me have my own opinions. They see my
opinions, but they will not understand them. I wish they could
see my points of view, but they cannot.[1]

Many social workers have trouble communicating with
teen-agers. When the counseling involves human sexuality and contraceptive use, the problem is compounded.
The first step to effective communication may be acknowl-
edging the counselor's own discomfort. The social worker
must recognize that a teen-ager may be apprehensive because of previous negative experiences with counselors.
The worker must, therefore, allow time to dispel past
stereotypes. To facilitate a satisfactory helping relationship, it is advisable to discuss teen-age problems not directly related to human sexuality or contraception, until

1. Robert C. Sorensen, *Adolescent Sexuality in Contemporary America. Personal Values and Sexual Behavior. Ages 13–19* (New York: World
Publishing Company, 1973), p. 66.

trust is established. This procedure will open channels of communication and help the worker learn something about the client that will be useful later in the relationship.

Effective communication must include discussion of various aspects of sexual behavior and sexual functions in terms that the teen-ager can understand. It is often helpful in the beginning stages of counseling to ask the client what words she uses and to use the terms which the client suggests if these words are not offensive. In this context, "offensive" is not a value judgment, but should reflect the worker's concern that discussion of sex and contraception be directed toward healthy acceptance of normal activities. Words that degrade sex and the human body are counterproductive. Common words and phrases which do help discussion include womb, cramps, period, sleeping or having sex with someone, and nature.

In the course of counseling, it is a good idea to stop occasionally and ask the client if he or she understands what you are trying to explain. Negative responses, silence, or puzzled reactions indicate that there is a need for simplification or further explanation. If the client replies that he or she does understand, it is helpful to ask him or her to repeat, in his or her own words, what has been said. This request is one way of determining what the client has actually learned. It also encourages questions on the part of an insecure or uncertain client.[2]

Resistances to contraception

Helping professionals who counsel teen-agers recognize some syndromes which lead to such tragedies as unwanted pregnancies, neglected children born to mothers unprepared for parental responsibilities, and couples forced into marriage doomed to failure.

The "moral" teen-age syndrome. Adolescents who equate the planned use of contraceptives with promiscu-

2. Mary Love, "Contraception for Adolescents," *Family Planning Perspectives*, 5, (Winter 1973).

ity or with intended sexual intercourse are often ambivalent about the use of a birth control method. They do not want to become pregnant and feel that sex outside of marriage is wrong. Even when they find themselves in relationships in which sexual intercourse is likely to result, they feel that unprotected intercourse is more moral because it just happened. The premeditation involved in going to a clinic to obtain a method of birth control arouses great feelings of guilt about sexual feelings. Often, teenagers who have been pregnant before feel strongly that they have "learned their lesson" and that it will "never happen again."

Counseling these teen-agers by drawing upon their own strong moral sense is often successful. By helping them understand that unprotected intercourse is more irresponsible than the use of contraceptives, these teenagers frequently become conscientious contraceptors.

The "It can't happen to me" syndrome. This attitude is frequently found among teen-agers who started sexual activity soon after menses began, without realizing that there is a period of about three years after the onset of menstruation when pregnancy is less likely. Therefore, it is hard to convince them that they are now vulnerable to unwanted conception. A rational explanation of the facts of early low fecundity, the exact periods of safe intercourse, and the probability of pregnancy (about 80 percent in a twelve-month period of unprotected regular intercourse) may have some effect.[3] A few questions about what they really want from life may also help them realize what their alternative choices are.

The sexual victim pattern. Many rather passive adolescent girls find themselves engaging in sexual relations which they neither seek nor enjoy. Frequently, their partners are older than they and only casually involved with the girls, but are sophisticated enough to pressure them

3. Constance Conrad, Robert Hatcher, and Ted Simon, *Contraceptive Technology* (Atlanta: Emory University School of Medicine, 1972).

into sexual unions. Most of these girls know very little about sexuality or contraceptives and are afraid to ask. The social worker may succeed if she assumes a supportive role, helping such a girl to realize that she does not have to submit to sexual exploitation in order to be accepted, and showing her that pregnancy can be avoided. Strong casework support may also be needed to help her overcome apprehensions and utilize family planning services. Passive teen-agers are often more interested in using the intrauterine device (IUD) form of contraception; thus protected, they should receive further supportive and therapeutic counseling concerning their sexual development and identity.

The "I want to be pregnant" syndrome. Many social workers express surprise at the number of adolescents who verbalize a desire for pregnancy. Some wish only to experience pregnancy and do not want to have a baby. Others want children, even though to mature observers they do not seem either ready for or capable of responsible parenthood. The social worker is faced with the difficult task of helping the teen-ager examine her motivations for desiring pregnancy, while attempting to ensure that she has contraceptive protection as this exploration is taking place.

Problems of referral

Even for adolescents who desire contraception and do not have any particular problems which would prevent their successful use of it, the thought of going to a family planning clinic may cause anxiety and guilt.[4] In referring a teen-ager for contraception, the social worker should explain clinic procedures in detail, questions the client may expect to be asked, and how she will be treated. Many clinics will not publicize the fact that they provide contraceptive services for teen-agers and, therefore, fail to legiti-

4. Sadja Goldsmith et al. "Teen-agers, Sex and Contraception," *Family Planning Perspectives,* 4:32–38 (January 1972).

mize the service. This problem is magnified when clinics require parental consent or insist that unwed adolescents undergo intensive counseling, suggesting that their sexual activity is pathological. Any negative feelings or expereiences teen-agers might have about clinic attendance should be discussed openly so that the young client can accept and cope with her reactions.

It is helpful for the counselor to discuss alternatives before a method is chosen. Although the physician will explain a method when it has been prescribed, the counselor can repeat the explanation after a method has been selected. This latter step will encourage questions by the client which were not asked at the time of the examination. An explanation by the counselor will also help clarify directions for the use of contraceptives available without a doctor's prescription.

The vicissitudes of adolescent love affairs have important implications for contraceptive use. Adolescent relations tend to be less permanent than those of adults, and breakups often result in cessation of use of contraceptives. This situation is understandable, although the adolescent should be encouraged to resume birth control whenever he or she anticipates becoming sexually active in the future. Research indicates that adolescent contraceptors are accepting of themselves as people and sexual beings and have higher aspirations for themselves than do those who have problems with unwanted pregnancies or contraceptive continuation.[5] The counselor who reinforces self-acceptance will also enhance conception control.

Basic Counseling Guidelines

The social worker who provides contraceptive counseling to teen-agers has a major task. She must convince both parents and teen-agers that sexual activity involves a dual

5. William L. Graves, and Barbara R. Bradshaw, "Early Reconception and Contraceptive Use Among Black Teen-age Girls After an Illegitimate Birth," *American Journal of Public Health* 65:738–40, (July 1975).

responsibility; to the participants and to unborn children. Responsible sex means that the persons involved take precautions to prevent pregnancies which are neither desirable nor convenient for either party at that time. Dr. Sol Gordon points out that every culture has some moral code. Teen-agers want and need sensible guidelines in this very emotionally charged area. The guidelines Dr. Gordon offers young people include:

1. No one has the right to exploit another person's body, commercially or sexually; do not have sex with anyone who does not care about you.

2. No one has the right to bring unwanted children into the world; no sex without birth control.

3. No one has the right to spread venereal disease; seek medical treatment first.

4. No one has the right to impose his sexual preferences on anyone else, including when, where and with whom to have sex; sexual choices must be voluntary.

5. No sex until *you* feel ready.[6]

6. Sol Gordon, *Newsletter* (Syracuse, N. Y.: Family Planning and Population Information Center), 1973.

VI

CONTRACEPTIVE TECHNOLOGY

14

Physician-Related Methods of Birth Control

From a medical standpoint, oral contraceptives have been in use only a relatively short time and the intrauterine device (IUD) an even shorter time. The emergence of a second generation of IUD's will undoubtedly bring with it a new set of contraindications and complications that have not yet been discovered. All of the physician-related methods of contraception carry with them underlying elements of risk; the risks vary depending on the population which uses the method and the training and skill of the physicians or practitioners who are dispensing the method. This entire subject is one of considerable controversy among both lay and legislative bodies; new restrictions and new contraindications appear almost daily. A continuous process of balancing the risk-benefit ratio is in progress. The latest contraceptive gadgetry is not necessarily the best simply because it seems to be easier to use or appears to answer an individual's particular problem. It is safe to say that by the time this publication reaches the hands of the reader certain portions of it will have become obsolete.

The following chapters are intended as a basic introduction to contraceptive technology for social workers and other counselors. In certain instances, terms and processes have been simplified, and should not be considered medically definitive. For more detailed information, counselors are urged to develop a good consulting relationship with a physician, clinic, or a nurse practitioner who is solidly trained in the field of clinical contraceptive work and contraceptive technology.

Oral Contraceptives

How They Work: Pills prevent pregnancy primarily by preventing eggs from being released from the ovaries. When no egg is released, a woman cannot become pregnant.

*Theoretical And Use Effectiveness: If one hundred women use the pills correctly for one year, less than one woman will become pregnant. In actual use studies, about sixteen became pregnant.

Side Effects: Main serious side effects are blood clotting disorders and high blood pressure. Less serious side effects include small weight gain, nausea, breast tenderness or enlargement, and fluid retention.

Medical Contraindications: A history of cancer of the breast or reproductive tract, blood clots, varicose veins, kidney disease, undiagnosed vaginal bleeding, hypertension, liver disease, diabetes, thrombophleblitis, sickle cell anemia, and patients of more than age forty.

Practical Contraindications: Disorganized patients who would be unable to follow a pill regimen; patients who might have difficulty in obtaining a steady supply of pills: and teen-agers subject to family or peer pressures which might interfere with the use of the pill.

Indications for Use:	Oral contraceptives are very effective contraceptives and are highly recommended when contraindications do not exist. In some instances oral contraceptives are used to treat specific causes of menstrual pain.
Special Note:	Counsel any client on oral contraceptives to see a doctor immediately if she has severe headaches, blurred vision, leg pains, or chest pains. In fact, the patient should be warned to consult her physician or clinic immediately if she has anxiety or feelings of loss of well-being while on the pills. A client should be urged not to stop the pill on her own, but only on the advice of the physician or nurse practitioner, who will be able to prescribe another method to avoid unwanted pregnancy while her complication is being investigated. On the other hand, she should not wait to see if these problems go away; they may be symptoms of serious side effects of these potent hormones.

*Theoretical effectiveness refers to statistical probabilities based on continued, correct usage. Use effectiveness refers to documentation based on actual results, including incorrect usage.

Mechanism of Action. Birth control pills contain various combinations of synthetic female hormones: estrogen, progesterone, or the two in combination. These synthetic hormones duplicate the higher levels of natural hormones produced by the body during pregnancy or during the menstrual cycle. The hormone levels are manipulated according to the plan of the particular pill to prevent maturation and release of an egg from the ovary (ovulation) and to create a climate within the uterine cavity and the cervix which is hostile to the survival of fertilizing sperm, or to the implantation of a fertilized ovum if fertilization should occur.

Birth control pills may be divided into three general groups: combination, sequential, or single hormone (minipill) preparations. The combination pills combine synthetic estrogen and progesterone in varying dosages, depending upon the manufacturer and the particular dosage manufactured. These pills, for the most part, act to produce a false pregnancy reaction in the patient and thereby accomplish the effects described above. When prescribed the combination pill, the patient takes the same combination of hormones for a twenty-one-day period of time without alterations in dosage.

The sequential pills are devised to simulate the normal ovarian cycle; thus the sequential pill provides estrogen alone for the first fourteen to fifteen days and then progesterone plus estrogen for the final several days of the cycle. These pills depend on estrogen alone for the suppression of the egg-producing function of the ovary and, therefore, more estrogen is supplied than is present in the combination pills.

The minipills have been in use in the United States since January 1973. These pills are designed to provide a small but continuing dose of progesterone throughout the entire cycle, including the time of the menstrual period. The patient is required to take one pill per day indefinitely. Because pregnancy rates are highest during the first six months of use of this method, clients should be advised to use a second contraceptive measure during that period of time.

Directions for Use. Because the combination pill is by far the most widely used oral contraceptive, this discussion will focus on the use of the combination pill only. Combination pills are packaged in two ways: (1) The first method of packaging consists of twenty-one pills, to be taken one per day at the same time daily, for twenty-one days; no pills are then taken for seven days, and a new package is started on the eighth day. During the week that no pills are taken menstruation usually occurs. (2) The second method consists of packages of twenty-eight pills, to be taken one per day for twenty-eight days, after which a new package cycle of pills is started. The last seven pills to be taken are of a color different from that of the contraceptive pills and are usually composed of an inert ingredient; in some formulations they may contain supplementary iron substances. These last seven pills need not be taken, as their primary function is to remind the patient of daily pill use. They should never be substituted for active pills. Menstruation will occur during the week that the inert pills are taken.

Side Effects. It must be remembered that the oral contraceptives are potent hormonal substances, and as such may have specific side effects in individual users. For the most part, these side effects can be divided into two classifications. First, the mild nonlife-threatening side effects such as nausea; vomiting; gastrointestinal symptoms, such as abdominal cramping or bloating; breakthrough bleeding; spotting, change in menstrual flow; edema; changes in skin pigmentation, cholasma, or white spots on the skin, or melasma, or the formation of pigmented areas on the bridge of the nose and cheeks; breast tenderness, enlargement, and occasionally secretion; and increase in cervical erosions and cervical secretions causing increase in vaginal discharge, and minimal rises in blood pressure in susceptible individuals. Mental depression and psychosexual changes manifested by loss of sex urge have been reported in association with use of oral contraception. It is most important that the client be informed that these mild side effects are for the most part transitory and will disappear after several cycles of use. In some instances, the anxiety produced by these symptoms may be strong enough to cause the client to cease using the oral contraceptive. Clients should be urged to seek advice for an alternative method, or help in alleviating their anxiety before discontinuing use of the pills; discontinuation all too frequently results in an unplanned pregnancy.

The second classification of side effects associated with the use of oral contraception which occur in a small number of women are severe; the user should be alerted to the possibility of their occurrence. These side effects are related to alterations in blood clotting, such as formation of clots in the leg veins (thrombophlebitis). Occasionally, these clots may break off and be carried to the lung (pulmonary embolism), posing a real threat to the life of the user. Reported blood clotting alterations in the blood vessels of the brain, have resulted in stroke symptoms and marked disability, or death. Diseases of the brain and eye related either to blood clotting or to pressure changes have been reported. Recent studies have shown that women over forty who are users of oral contraceptives are at almost twice the risk of clotting defects of the blood vessel supplying the heart muscle (coronary thrombosis) as are non-users.

There is no proof of a direct cause and effect relationship between oral contraceptive use and precipitation of a cancer which does not already exist within the body. The use of oral contraceptives in cases of undiagnosed cancers of this type can, however, apparently increase the rate of the cancer growth and affect the prognosis of the course of the disease.

It should be strongly emphasized that these severe complications associated with oral contraception occur in very few patients among the large number of pill users. In a normal healthy woman, the very real maternal mortality is considerably higher than any mortality associated with pill use, making pregnancy still a more dangerous condition than the complications described in relation to oral contraception. However, in women over thirty-five or forty, particularly those who have had a number of pregnancies, the likelihood of preexisting varicose veins and latent diabetes or hypertension is considerably increased. Such patients would be better advised to use other methods of contraception than the pills and may prefer to undergo sterilization as a permanent form of contraception.

As with any other potent medication, oral contraceptives should only be prescribed under careful medical supervision, and the client should have available to her the means of periodic followup throughout the time that she is taking oral contraceptives.

Medical Contraindications. Oral contraceptives are not recommended for use by women with a history of blood clotting, cancer of the breast or reproductive system, kidney infection or hepatitis, undiagnosed vaginal bleeding, thrombophlebitis, hypertension, or sickle cell anemia. Women with diabetes, epilepsy, migraine headaches, asthma, or severe depression may use oral contraceptives only under strict medical supervision. Oral contraceptive users should be advised to watch for severe leg cramps, vascular headaches, blurred vision, and chest pains, and to report them to their physicians immediately. In addition, any abrupt change in health status, such as injury or severe infection, may increase the danger of abnormal blood clooting.

Practical Contraindications. Women who have mixed feelings about contraception, or who are emotionally distrubed or mentally deficient are not apt to be successful in the use of oral contraceptives. The daily dosage schedule requires strong motivation. The woman who is in a stable sexual relationship in which the timing and frequency of coitus is predictable is usually better motivated to routine pill taking than the woman whose sexual encounters are more casual and unpredictable. In addition, women in isolated rural areas, or of marginal economic status may not have access to a continuing supply of pills.

Indications for Use. The pill is among the most effective methods for the prevention of pregnancy. It is relatively inexpensive, generally available, and easy to use. When there are no contraindications for its use, it is highly recommended.

Intrauterine Device (IUD)

How It Works: Nobody knows. It is probably that the device prevents the fertilized egg from implanting in the uterus.

Theoretical and Use Effectiveness:	If one hundred women use the IUD correctly for one year, one to three will get pregnant. In actual use studies, about six get pregnant.
Side Effects:	Cramps after insertion; longer, heavier menstrual bleeding, especially in first few cycles following insertion.
Medical Contraindications:	Heavy menstrual flow or cramping, pelvic inflammatory disease, venereal disease, undiagnosed vaginal bleeding, pregnancy.
Practical Contradictions:	Presence of IUD strings in vagina must be confirmed regularly. Some women will not put their fingers in their vagina.
Indications for Use:	Highly recommended; a very effective method which requires little effort on the part of users after initial insertion. Especially recommended for women who do not like or are not likely to keep to a daily regimen.
Special Note:	A few family planning programs now counsel IUD patients to use an additional method of birth control, such as condoms or foam, at midcycle, to improve the chances of avoiding pregnancy. Pregnancy in the presence of an IUD is a serious complication which may lead to severe infection and even death. Recently, there have been reports of cases of fatal infection, with sepsis and pelvic abscess resulting in the removal of the pelvic organs as a result of IUD's in situ in pregnancy.

The intrauterine device (IUD) is a small object which is inserted into the uterus through the vagina. IUD's come in a variety of shapes and sizes, are designed to remain in place until the woman desires pregnancy, and should be removed only by a physician or other trained clinician.

Until recently, the IUD was generally recommended for use only by women who had already had a child. Nulliparous women, especially teen-agers, often experienced severe cramping and bleeding as their bodies tried to adjust to the device. Now, however, specially sized IUD's are being used increasingly by teen-agers or older women who have had no children. The insertion of the IUD (usually two days after the onset of menstrual bleeding) is a quick and relatively safe procedure, although some discomfort is usually felt. Some women may experience dizziness or fainting as a result of the dilation of the cervix. A paracervical block at the time of insertion can eliminate the pain. After insertion, the woman should be instructed to check the string attached to the IUD once or twice a month, particularly after the menstrual period, to be sure it is in place.

Mechanism of Action. Ancient camel drivers knew that peach pits inserted in a camel's uterus would prevent her from becoming pregnant during long trips through the desert. Despite its long history, however, exactly how an IUD functions to prevent pregnancy is not known. Researchers postulate that the IUD prevents pregnancy by irritating the lining of the uterus, thus preventing implantation of the fertilized egg; perhaps the IUD speeds the egg through the fallopian tube so that it reaches the uterus before the endometrium is properly developed to receive it, or perhaps it causes hormonal changes which suppress ovulation.[1]

Directions for Use. Since most pregnancies with IUD's occur within the first month after insertion, it is recommended that a back-up method of contraception be used in conjunction with the IUD during this period. Because the uterus may occasionally expel the IUD, the user should be instructed to check occasionally the small

1. Advisory Committee on Obstetrics and Gynecology, *Report on Intrauterine Contraceptive Devices* (Washington, D.C.: U.S. Department of Health, Education, and Welfare, January 1968).

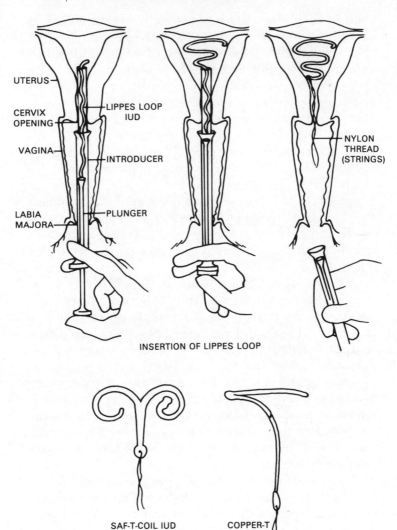

UTERUS

CERVIX
OPENING

VAGINA

LIPPES LOOP
IUD

INTRODUCER

LABIA
MAJORA

PLUNGER

NYLON
THREAD
(STRINGS)

INSERTION OF LIPPES LOOP

SAF-T-COIL IUD   COPPER-T

OTHER COMMONLY USED IUDS

strings attached to the device to ensure that it is properly in place. This step is especially important during the first few months following insertion. If it is not in place, she should contact a family planning clinic or private physician at once so that it can be replaced or adjusted. A back-up method of birth control should be used until the IUD is properly placed.

Side Effects. Most users experience some cramping as the uterus adjusts to the IUD. Some women report spotting and increased menstrual flow. Most of these effects disappear as the uterus becomes accustomed to the device, usually within two to three months. On rare occasions, the uterus is perforated upon insertion of an IUD, usually due to a lack of skill on the part of the physician.

Medical Contraindications for Use. Women with excessively heavy menstrual flow or cramping, pelvic inflammatory disease, venereal disease, vaginal or uterine infection, or undiagnosed vaginal bleeding should not use an IUD.

Practical Contraindications for Use. Women who have strong negative feelings about touching their sexual organs should be carefully counseled before the decision is made to insert an IUD. Such women may be unlikely to check inside the vagina for the strings attached to the device to determine proper placement.

Indications for Use. The IUD is a safe and very reliable means of contraception. Although the theoretical effectiveness of the IUD is somewhat lower than that of the pill, its use effectiveness is higher than that of the pill. It is recommended for women who cannot or do not want to use oral contraceptives. It is also recommended for women whose age and sporadic sexual activity do not merit the use of oral contraceptives, and for women who prefer a method of contraception that requires little effort on their part.

Diaphragm with Spermicidal Jelly or Cream

How It Works:	The diaphragm works in two ways: mechanical barrier to sperm, chemicals in the jelly or cream kill sperm.
Theoretical And Use Effectiveness:	If one hundred women use the combination of diaphragm and jelly correctly for one year, two or three will get pregnant. In actual use studies eight to thirty-three get pregnant.
Side Effects:	Allergy to rubber or chemical in cream or jelly.
Medical Contraindications:	Not recommended for women with vaginal infection, cysts; uterine displacement, short rigid, inelastic vaginal walls, or marked vaginal relaxation; or for women who have delivered many large babies, or have had vaginal surgery.
Practical Contraindications:	Aversion to touching one's own genitals. Many physicians, especially in public clinics, do not have the time or skills to instruct patients in the use of the diaphragm. Users often use diaphragms without the jelly. When used improperly in this fashion, pregnancies rise to thirty-eight for every hundred women.
Indications for Use	When other contraceptives are contraindicated; in most women, the diaphragm is a medically safe method for those who learn to insert and use it properly.

The diaphragm is one of the oldest and, until recently, most frequently used methods of contraception. The diaphragm first came into use in 1887.[2] It consists of a flat, narrow, spring steel band forming a ring. Vulcanized latex rubber completely covers the steel ring, forming a shallow

2. John Peel and Malcolm Potts, *Textbook of Contraceptive Practice* (Cambridge: Cambridge University Press, 1970), p. 62.

cup. The original design, with few modifications, has remained virtually unchanged until today. Diaphragms come in sizes from fifty to one hundred-five millimeters in diameter, in variations of five millimeters. The most common size is between seventy and eighty millimeters. The size needed is determined by the number of children a woman has had; a physician must determine the correct size for a woman.

Mechanism of Action. The diaphragm holds spermicidal jelly or cream against the cervix, blocking the entry of the sperm into the uterus and killing the sperm. The diaphragm is not a highly effective contraceptive when used without jelly or cream, because sperm, being very small and mobile, can swim around the rim and through the cervix.

Directions for Use. One teaspoon of spermicidal jelly or cream, specifically made for use with diaphragms, is applied to the interior surface of the diaphragm both in the center and around the rim. The diaphragm should be inserted not more than six hours before intercourse by squeezing the opposite sides of the rim together and, with one leg raised, directing the diaphragm down against the posterior wall of the vagina as far as it will go. The rim of the diaphragm is then tucked up behind the pelvic bone. The user should feel her cervix through the latex to make sure that the diaphragm is properly positioned. The diaphragm should not be removed until at least six hours after the last act of intercourse, to make sure that all sperm in the vagina are dead. It may be left in place for as long as twenty-four hours. Douching is not necessary. Removal is effected by hooking a finger behind the rim and pulling it down and out. After use, the diaphragm should be washed with soap and warm water, rinsed, dried, and dusted with talcum powder. It should periodically be tested for perforations by filling it with warm water and watching for leaks.

The diaphragm should be replaced or refitted under certain conditions: the discovery of perforations, worn

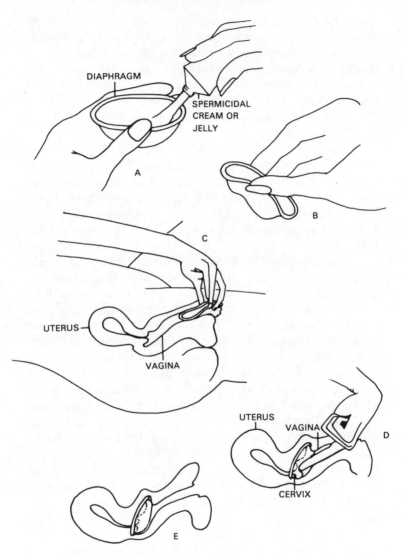

STEPS IN INSERTING THE DIAPHRAGM

spots, or other defects; recent birth of a child, because the vagina is stretched during childbirth; weight loss or gain of more than fifteen pounds; and after the initial several weeks of intercourse for women who get fitted before becoming sexually active. For extra protection, the diaphragm should be replaced after six months of normal use.

Side Effects. Some women are allergic to particular brands of spermicidal jellies or creams. Another brand of jelly can usually be substituted satisfactorily.

Medical Contraindications for Use. The diaphragm is not recommended for women with vaginal infections or cysts; uterine displacement or marked vaginal relaxation; previous vaginal surgery; or short, rigid, or inelastic vaginal walls. In some women who have had a number of large babies, the vagina may be so stretched that the diaphragm may slip badly during the plateau phase of sexual excitement, making the diaphragm almost totally useless.

Practical Contraindications for Use. Women must be highly motivated to use this method of contraception. Considerable time and effort are involved in learning and continuing its use. As with the IUD, women with an aversion to handling their genitals are less likely to be successful with this method. Many young doctors do not know how to fit a diaphragm properly or how to instruct the patient in its use. Many physicians, especially those serving the medically indigent, are unwilling or unable to take the time to teach the patient how to use this contraceptive method. In spite of these problems, the use of the diaphragm is undergoing a resurgence among women who do not want to use oral contraception.

Indications for Use. The diaphragm with spermicidal jelly or cream is fairly reliable and has no harmful side effects on the user's body. Because it can be inserted several hours before intercourse, foreplay need not be interrupted.

Depo-Provera*

How It Works: Prevents eggs from being released from the ovaries.

Theoretical and Use Effectiveness: If one hundred women receive Depo-Provera injections correctly for one year, less than one will get pregnant. In actual studies, five to ten get pregnant.

Side Effects: Heavy menstrual bleeding, breakthrough bleeding, headaches, absence of menstrual periods, weight gain, decreased sex drive, potential sterility.

Medical Contraindications: Should be used only by women who are sure they want no more children. There is a possibility of permanent sterility associated with this drug.

Practical Contraindications: Not in use in most areas of the country.

Indications for Use: High parity for women who desire no more children, are mentally incompetent, or are unlikely to use other methods.

*Depo-Provera has been officially approved three times by the Food and Drug Administration, and approval has been withdrawn twice. The last recall was in November 1974, resulting from some indications of linkage with cancer. It has since been reapproved (November, 1975) for use with a signed consent form.

Mechanism of Action. A woman using this method gets an injection every three months. Depo-Provera is a form of progesterone which remains active for three months after injection. Similar to oral contraceptives, it prevents ovulation and renders the cervical mucus hostile to sperm, thereby preventing fertilization.

Directions for Use. The woman must return to the clinic or physician for an injection every three months. If she develops side effects, she should return immediately for medical assistance.

Side Effects. Among the side effects caused by this drug

are excessive bleeding, breakthrough bleeding, cessation of menses, headaches, excessive weight gain, decreased libido, and, possibly, permanent sterility.

Medical Contraindications for Use. Because of the possibility of permanent sterility, this drug is not recommended for women desiring children at some future time.

Practical Contraindications for Use. Because the Federal Food and Drug Administration has fluctuated regarding the approval of Depo-Provera, it may be difficult to obtain.

Indications for Use. Depo-Provera may be used by women who are awaiting sterilization and do not wish to use other methods of birth control before the operation. Women with large families who do not want, or cannot yet obtain, sterilization often prefer Depo-Provera to other forms of contraception. It is a commonly used method of contraception for the mentally retarded and the mentally ill.

Post-Intercourse Methods of Birth Control

These methods cannot be classified either as contraceptive or as abortifacients. They are used following unprotected sexual intercourse when pregnancy is suspected, but before it is possible to establish that fact. For this reason, such methods are often called presumptive abortion or menstrual regulation. Both methods discussed are relatively new, and the long-range effects have not been fully studied. Neither should be used on a regular or routine basis as a substitute for a tested method of birth control. Both, however, will probably become important back-up methods when regular contraceptive techniques have not been used, and they are less expensive and less traumatic than an abortion might be. In cases of rape or incest, such methods are routinely used in many hospitals.

Many low-income women are not aware of the existence of post-coital (post-intercourse) methods of birth control. The argument that such methods should not be discussed because they are not medically proven involves the assumption that counselors are better requipped to make decisions for their clients than their clients are to make decisions for themselves. It is generally recommended that:

1. To keep a client in ignorance is unfair and judgmental. Women should be aware of all options open to them.

2. Clients should be informed of the disadvantages and side effects of these methods, as well as the positive aspects.

3. If there are no medical contraindications, the use of these or any other methods should be primarily the decision of the client.

The Morning-After Pill (Diethylstilbesterol)

How It Works:	It is believed that changes in the lining of the uterus prevent the implantation of the fertilized egg.
Theoretical and Use Effectiveness:	Over 99 percent effective if administered within seventy-two hours after unprotected intercourse. Should the method fail, however, abortion should be offered as an alternative.
Side Effects:	Extreme nausea and vomiting, vaginal spotting, diarrhea; some evidence of genital cancer in female offspring of pregnant women who take the drug and continue the pregnancy.
Medical Contraindications:	Same as for oral contraceptives.
Practical Contraindications:	Long-range studies of effects have not been undertaken; extreme nausea makes it undesirable except as an emergency measure.
Indications for Use:	In emergency situations, especially in cases of rape or incest and unprotected mid-cycle intercourse.

Mechanism of Action. The morning-after pill is made up of a high-dosage synthetic estrogen called Diethylstilbesterol (stilbesterol). It prevents the already fertilized egg from implanting in the uterus and developing. The exact mechanism by which the fertile egg is prevented from implanting in the uterine lining can only be postulated. It is theorized that the drug accelerates or slows down the passage of the egg through the fallopian tube, changes the surface of the uterine lining, or changes the hormone production of the ovaries. Whatever the exact mechanism of action, there is evidence to show that implantation of the egg is averted and pregnancy prevented.

Directions for Use. Diethylstilbesterol is a powerful drug and should be administered only under medical supervision. It should be taken within seventy-two hours of unprotected mid-cycle intercourse and, if possible, within forty-eight hours. The drug is administered for five days, either in pill or injectable form. Since Diethylstilbesterol may stimulate ovulation if it has not already occurred before the drug is taken, unprotected exposure to intercourse must be avoided.

Knowledge of the ovulatory cycle is essential if women are to calculate when they are most likely to become pregnant following unprotected intercourse. Also, women should be told where they can receive Diethylstilbesterol treatment. Planned Parenthood affiliates and other family planning clinics have the names of physicians and hospitals where such treatment can be obtained. Because administration of the drug must begin very shortly after intercourse, the education and counseling process must often be carried out before the fact, as part of general contraceptive counseling.

Side Effects. Nausea, vomiting, headaches, vaginal spotting, diarrhea, increased or decreased menses, and bloated or swollen conditions have been reported. Many physicians have been prescribing stilbesterol for private patients for years, but the drug received FDA approval for use on an emergency basis only in 1973.[3] Higher dosages have also been used over many years to prevent miscarriages in pregnant women. When the drug is used for this purpose, there is documentation that vaginal cancer may occur in 50 percent of exposed female offspring when they reach adolescence. It is for this reason that many physicians hesitate to use the drug.[4] Although it is thought to be more than 99 percent effective, abortion should be offered as an option in the rare instances when a woman proves to be pregnant following administration of Diethylstilbesterol.

Medical Contraindications for Use. The morning-after pill should not be used by any woman displaying contraindications for oral contraceptive use.

Practical Contraindications for Use. The morning-after pill is not to be considered a contraceptive for continued usage. It is a powerful drug which may induce many unpleasant, if not harmful, side effects, and it therefore should be used only in emergency situations. Some medical facilities will refuse to administer the drug more than once to anyone seeking it.

Indications for Use. The morning-after pill is an effective emergency means of preventing pregnancy due to unprotected mid-cycle intercourse. It is routinely administered to rape cases in hospital emergency rooms. Due to the evidence of genital cancer in the female offspring of pregnant women who use the drug, it should never be administered to any woman who is not first counseled on the advisability of abortion should the pregnancy continue.

3. "FDA Approves DES, Urges Limited Use," *Family Planning Digest,* 2:12 (May 1973).
4. John Morris and Gertrude Van Wagonen, "Interception: The Use of Post Ovulatory Estrogens to Prevent Implantation," *American Journal of Obstetrics and Gynecology,* 115:101–06 (January 1973).

Minisuction

How It Works: Menstruation is induced by suction extraction of the endometrial lining normally discharged during menstruation, thereby preventing the implantation of a possibly fertilized egg.

Theoretical and Use Effectiveness: Almost completely effective, but long-term studies have not yet been done.

Side Effects: Cramping and bleeding; rarely severe cramping and other symptoms described in section on vacuum curettage.

Medical Contraindications: Same as with vacuum curettage.

Practical Contraindications: The long-range effects are not yet known, so regular use of this technique as a contraceptive is inadvisable.

Indications for Use: After exposure to unprotected mid-cycle intercourse, especially in cases of incest or rape.

Mechanism of Action. Minisuction (also called presumptive abortion, a traumatic termination, menstrual regulation, and menstrual extraction) is a relatively new method of contraception which is likely to be more commonly used in the future. It is actually a presumptive abortion, in that the patient is assumed to be pregnant although it is too early to tell through a pregnancy test. Minisuction can be performed from the first week after the first missed period to no later than the seventh week from the first day of the woman's last period.[5] Suspected pregnancy is prevented by inducing menstruation through suction. This operation can be done simply and with few problems as an office procedure.

5. *Atraumatic Termination of Pregnancy: A Medical Protocol* (New York: National Women's Health Coalition, 1973).

Procedure. The procedure is begun when the woman is given a pelvic examination and a pregnancy test to determine that she is not over the pregnant seven week limit. (If the test is positive, she is probably over the seven week period and another method is used.) The speculum is inserted and a local anesthesia (paracervical block) is given if indicated, (for example, if the woman has not had a baby in the past or if she has had previous Cesarean sections). A small hollow instrument like a drinking straw (cannula) is inserted through the cervical opening into the uterus. The suction is turned on and the cannula is rotated gently until the endometrial lining normally shed during menstruation is extracted. The operation will take less than a minute to complete from this point.

Side Effects. The woman will probably experience menstrual-type cramping during the procedure, but it should disappear within five minutes after the operation. She will be able to resume normal activity immediately, but may experience bleeding from one to ten days after the minisuction. The woman's next menstruation will occur four to five weeks after the procedure. Contraception should be used to prevent pregnancy in the next cycle.[6]

Complications. A woman may feel faint or complain of severe cramps after the minisuction. If she does, she should remain at the office or facility until she begins to feel better. This reaction usually lasts about fifteen or twenty minutes.

Further, if a woman does not menstruate within five weeks after the procedure, a pregnancy test should be done to determine whether the minisuction failed to terminate the pregnancy. Finally, the woman should be informed of the symptoms regarding infections described in the section on vacuum curettage in the chapter on abortions.

Proponents of this method claim it can be performed

6. Malcolm Potts and H. Karman, "Very Early Abortion Using Syringe as Vacuum Form," *Lancet*, 1972, p. 1051.

on a regular basis, even monthly. The more cautious maintain that until there are more data from clinical trials, minisuction should not be used as a routine procedure to induce bleeding, although it is certainly less physically traumatic than other procedures.

15.

Nonprescription Methods of Birth Control

The Condom (Rubber, Prophylactic)

How It Works: Mechanical barrier. Prevents sperm from being deposited in vagina.

Theoretical and Use Effectiveness: If 100 couples use only condoms correctly for one year, about two women will get pregnant. Actual use studies show that 11–28 women will get pregnant.

Side Effects: Occasional allergy to rubber. Condoms made of animal membrane may be substituted.

Medical Contraindications: None

Practical Contraindications: If distasteful to one or both partners, the couple need to be motivated to make using the condom part of foreplay.

Indications for Use: When other more effective methods are contraindicated; easily carried and used by a male who is only occasionally sexually active; a prevention against veneral disease.

Special Note: The condom is the only method of contraception which prevents spread of venereal disease. Using foam in addition to condoms cuts actual pregnancies to five per year per 100 couples.

Mechanism of Action. The condom is a thin sheath of latex rubber or animal membrane worn over the erect penis during intercourse. It serves as a physical barrier to the transmission of sperm into the vagina. Condoms are available in many varieties, either dry or lubricated, in different colors, and with or without a reservoir tip. Condoms made of animal membrane are called "skins." They can be used by men allergic to latex rubber, offer increased sensitivity and transmission of heat, are less likely to break, and are more expensive than latex condoms.

Besides providing contraception, condoms have two secondary benefits. They serve as an effective protection against the transmission of venereal disease. Also, because they diminish sensation slightly, they can benefit men who suffer from premature ejaculation.

Directions for Use. The condom should be rolled over the erect penis before any vaginal contact is initiated. If

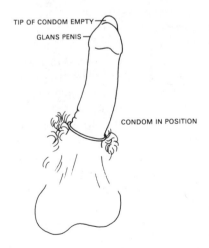

TIP OF CONDOM EMPTY

GLANS PENIS

CONDOM IN POSITION

there is no reservoir tip, a space should be left at the end to catch the semen and prevent the condom from bursting. If lubrication is needed, a water-soluble sterile lubricant may be used. Immediately after ejaculation, the condom should be grasped at the base to prevent spillage and the penis withdrawn. The condom should then be checked for any tears or leakage. If there has been leakage, even on the outer surfaces of the vagina, a spermicidal agent such as foam should be used immediately. It is a good idea to apply foam or jelly before using the condom as an extra precautionary measure. Condoms have a shelf life of about two years and should not be used thereafter.

Medical Contraindications for Use: No contraindications are present.

Practical Contraindications for Use. Men with limited potency, particularly older men, may have decreased potency because of decreased sensitivity through the use of the condom. In such situations there is often a tendency to remove the condom and proceed with unprotected intercourse.

The fact that the condom must be put on before intercourse may interfere with the spontaneity of the sex act. Many couples circumvent this possibility by incorporating application of the condom into their foreplay.

Very inexpensive condoms, such as those dispensed from gas station and rest-room vending machines, are inferior to better-known brands. They are more likely to have defects which can cause them to break during use. Condoms which cover only the tip of the penis, known as "caps" or "stubs," should be avoided because they can easily leak or slip out of place.

Indications for Use. Condoms are relatively inexpensive and easy to obtain. They can easily be carried in wallet or purse, although body heat may decompose the rubber over time. They are ideal for those persons whose pattern of sporadic sexual contacts makes the use of any of the physician-related contraceptives unlikely. Condoms are especially popular among teen-agers.

Spermicidal Vaginal Preparations

How They Work: Mechanical barrier to sperm; also contain chemicals which kill sperm.

Theoretical and Use Effectiveness: If 100 women use foam correctly for a year, about five will get pregnant. Actual use studies show fifteen to twenty-five will get pregnant.

Side Effects: Occasional allergic reaction to chemical ingredients.

Medical Contraindications: None.

Practical Contraindications: Must be motivated to incorporate insertion into foreplay or to stop foreplay to insert foam before each act of intercourse.

Indications for Use: When more effective methods are contraindicated. Easily carried and used by the woman or girl who is only occasionally sexually active.

Special Note: Using condoms in addition to foam cuts actual use pregnancies to 5 percent per 100 women.

Mechanism of Action. Foam and other spermicidal creams and jellies form a base for chemical agents which kill sperm. This base and spermicidal agents create a protective barrier when inserted properly into the woman's vagina, in the area of the cervix.

Directions for Use. Women using these preparations should be aware of the following: The container (if foam) should be shaken well (twenty times). Two applications of foam are recommended within thirty minutes before the first act of intercourse; an additional application of foam or other agent should be used before each act of intercourse. Insertion should be high in the vagina, as close to the cervix as possible. A condom is recommended as a backup for this method of birth control. Douching after use is not

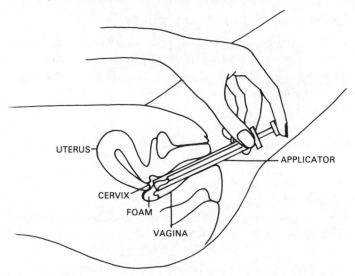

UTERUS

APPLICATOR

CERVIX

FOAM

VAGINA

INSERTION OF SPERMICIDAL FOAM, CREAM, OR JELLY WITHOUT DIAPHRAGM

necessary; if a woman wants to douche, she should wait at least six hours after the last intercourse.

Side Effects. These preparations may cause irritation to the vaginal area or the penis and may aggravate conditions of vaginitis or pelvic inflammatory disease.

Medical Contraindications for Use. No contraindications are present.

Practical Contraindications for Use. Insertion may interfere with the sex act unless incorporated into foreplay. Some women who do not like to touch their genitals may not accept this method of contraception.

Indications for Use. One advantage to spermicidals is that they may be purchased at a drugstore without a prescription. Foam may be purchased with a travel kit small enough to fit in a purse. Single dose applications, which look very much like a tampon, can also be purchased. Generally, spermicidal agents are relatively inexpensive and easy to use.

Douches

A common folk belief is that if the vagina is washed out with a special solution immediately after intercourse, sperm will be deactivated and pregnancy will be avoided. This method suffers from the defect of being too late to do much good; by the time the douche is started, sperm have had a chance to reach the uterus, where they can contact an egg. (Sperm can swim an inch in eight minutes, and almost half a billion sperm are normally ejaculated at each orgasm[1] Furthermore, the pressure of the douche can force concentrated sperm through the cervix, where they can effect fertilization. Because many women believe that douching works, a counselor should be able to explain the drawbacks of douching as a method of birth control.

Periodic Continence (Rhythm Method)

How It Works:	Intercourse is avoided during fertile days, so sperm are never able to reach a ripened egg.
Theoretical and Actual Effectiveness:	If 100 women use rhythm correctly for a year, fourteen will get pregnant. Actual use studies show that 38–40 women will get pregnant.
Side Effects:	Frustration. Unsafe period may last 8–21 days.
Medical Contraindications:	None
Practical Contraindications:	Most women cannot "read" their cycles accurately enough to use the rhythm method effectively enough. This is especially true of women with irregular cycles. Frustration may result.
Indications for Use:	For women with regular menstrual cycles and with medical, religious, moral, or prac-

1. Alan Guttmacher, *Birth Control and Love* (New York: Bantam Books, 1967), p. 9.

tical constraints contraindicating the use of other contraceptives.

Mechanism of Action. The rhythm method necessitates avoidance of sexual intercourse on those days during which the woman is fertile. In this way, sperm have no opportunity to unite with a mature egg. For the method to be effective, the woman must be able to determine her "unsafe" period, during which ovulation occurs. She must refrain from having sexual intercourse during this time unless she uses another means of birth control. The rhythm method has a poor reputation because of the problems of inaccuracy in pinpointing ovulation. Various techniques, which are described below, have been developed to increase accuracy in identifying ovulation in each cycle. They include recording basal temperature, observing cervical mucous discharge, making calendar calculations, and employing laboratory methods to determine hormone levels. The first three tell us only that ovulation has probably occurred. The last method is prohibitively expensive, except in instances of laboratory research or infertility treatment. Many women who want to use the rhythm method will need the help of a professional in calculating "safe" and "unsafe" periods.

1. Basal Body Temperature Method. This method of rhythm relies on checking a woman's basal body temperature (with a special thermometer with fine gradations) immediately after she wakens every morning.

The research behind this temperature method indicates that ovulation has an effect on a woman's basal body temperature. Immediately before ovulation, a woman's temperature drops. It rises again twenty-four hours after ovulation has occurred. In order to use this method, a woman must avoid unprotected intercourse until her temperature has remained elevated for three consecutive mornings. This abstinence is vital because the egg can live for three days after ovulation, and any contact with sperm during this time can cause pregnancy.

Utilizing the calendar method of determining the first day of the unsafe or fertile period is advisable because sometimes it is difficult to notice a drop in temperature which precedes ovulation. When the temperature rises and remains elevated for three consecutive days, it is theoretically safe to have intercourse. (It must be remembered that a woman's temperature can also rise due to tension or infections.)

2. *Cervical Mucus Observation.* The woman who does not have a cervical mucus loss is not ovulating. Following the menstrual period, the cervical mucus is scant and fairly liquid. It then becomes cloudy, white or yellowish, and of a sticky consistency. Over the next few days the mucus continues to be secreted, but becomes slippery, clear, and elastic just before the occurrence of ovulation.

Changes in the mucus tells a woman that she is going to ovulate soon. All sexual contact must be avoided on those days when the clear, elastic mucus is present. If the woman counts four days past the peak symptom days (last day of clear, slippery, elastic mucus discharge) she will have reached the late days of the cycle, and intercourse from that time until the end of the cycle should be safe. Some women have other physical symptoms of ovulation, such as slight spotting (bleeding) or pain in the lower abdomen or back. It should be noted that ovulatory discharges can be hidden by discharges caused by infections.

3. *Calendar Method.* To practice this method, a woman ideally should have a record of her menstrual periods over a year's time so that she can determine the length of her longest and shortest menstrual cycle. A menstrual cycle is the number of days from the first day of one month's menstruation to the first day of the next month's menstruation. Ovulation occurs approximately in the middle of each menstrual cycle. When calculating the fertile period, always count *the first day of menstrual bleeding* as day one of the cycle. The general formula for use is as follows: the number of days in the shortest cycle minus seventeen equals the last fertile day. Con-

TABLE 6   THE RHYTHM METHOD

How to Calculate the "Safe and "Unsafe" Days

Length of Shortest Period	First "Unsafe" Day After Start of any Period	Length of Longest Period	Last "Unsafe" Day After Start of Any Period
21 days	3rd day	21 days	10th day
22 days	4th day	22 days	11th day
23 days	5th day	23 days	12th day
24 days	6th day	24 days	13th day
25 days	7th day	25 days	14th day
26 days	8th day	26 days	15th day
27 days	9th day	27 days	16th day
28 days	10th day	28 days	17th day
29 days	11th day	29 days	18th day
30 days	12th day	30 days	19th day
31 days	13th day	31 days	20th day
32 days	14th day	32 days	21st day
33 days	15th day	33 days	22nd day
34 days	16th day	34 days	23rd day
35 days	17th day	35 days	24th day
36 days	18th day	36 days	25th day
37 days	19th day	37 days	26th day
38 days	20th day	38 days	27th day

This method of calculation assumes that ovulation occurs approximately twelve to sixteen days before a woman's next menstrual flow. Intercourse must be avoided two days before this five-day span and one day after to account for sperm and egg survival. For a woman with a regular menstrual cycle, the total theoretical fertile period is always eight days long.

sider all the days between the first fertile day and the last fertile day to be "unsafe" for having intercourse.

For example, if a woman's shortest cycle was twenty-eight days and longest cycle was thirty-one days, the eleventh day is the first "unsafe" day (twenty-eight minus seventeen) and the twentieth day is the last "unsafe" day (thirty-one minus eleven).

Medical Contraindications. No contraindications are present.

Practical Contraindications. Although there are no medical side effects directly related to the rhythm method of birth control, several disadvantages may be cited. First, if practiced correctly there is a likelihood that the man and woman will be frustrated because of long periods of abstinence; for a woman with a regular menstrual cycle, the total period of abstinence is eight days but if she has irregular cycles this period of abstinence can be much longer. This rigorous limitation of sexual intercourse requires that both partners be committed to avoiding the possibility of pregnancy and that they understand and be able to cope with the frustrations involved. Secondly, the method often does not work, particularly if menstrual cycles are not regular.

Indications for Use. Women who can note a pattern of regularity in the length of their menstrual cycles and who can notice definite physical symptoms of ovulation can expect some success if they determine their "unsafe" period and refrain from intercourse during that time. Positive attributes of this method are that it is free and that because it has the sanction of the Roman Catholic Church, many women who are strict adherents to that faith, may comfortably employ this method of birth control.

In the last analysis, when followed, any method of birth control is better than none at all. Abstinence can be used by a teen-ager who is only occasionally sexually active if she has regular cycles, if she has noticeable premenstrual symptoms, and if her menstrual periods last no longer than four to five days. She can have sexual intercourse with some safety during the four or five days of menstruation and the first few days before menstruation. It should also be noted that when carefully adhered to, the practice of the rhythm method reduces the number of acts of intercourse by one-third to one-half, thereby, almost by definition, reducing the likelihood of unwanted pregnancy.

TABLE 7   APPROXIMATE FAILURE RATE. (NUMBER OF
PREGNANCIES IN ONE HUNDRED WOMEN USING A
CONTRACEPTIVE FOR ONE YEAR)

	Theoretical Failure Rate	Actual Use Failure Rate
Abortion	0+	0+[a]
Abstinence	0	?
Hysterectomy	0.0001	0.0001
Tubal ligation	0.04	0.04
Vasectomy	Less than 0.15	0.15
Oral contraceptives (combined)	Less than 1.0	2–5[b]
I.M. Long-acting progestin	Less than 1.0	5–10
Condom, plus spermicidal agent	1.0	5
Low-dose oral progestin	1–4	5–10
IUD	1–5	6
Condom	3	15–20
Diaphragm	3	20–25
Spermicidal foam	3	30
Coitus interruptus	15	20–25
Rhythm (calendar method)	15	35
Lactation for twelve months	15	40[c]
Chance (sexually active)	80	80

[a]Among women actually depending upon abortion as a means of fertility control, effectiveness is less than 100 percent because in some instances women change their minds.

[b]Oral contraceptive failure rates may be far higher than this, if one considers women who become pregnant after discontinuing oral contraceptives, but prior to initiating another method. Oral contraceptive discontinuation rates of as high as 60 percent in the first year of use are not uncommon in family planning programs.

[c]Most women supplement breast feedings, significantly decreasing the contraceptive effectiveness of lactation. In Rwanda, 50 percent of non-lactating women were found to conceive by just over four months postpartum; among lactating women 50 percent had conceived at just over eighteen months postpartum (M. Bonte, and H. van Balen, Journal of Biosoc. Science 1: 97 (1969).

This table is adapted, with permission of the authors, from Robert A. Hatcher, et al., *Contraceptive Technology 1974-1975* (Atlanta, Georgia: Emory University Family Planning Program, Department of Gynecology and Obstetrics, Emory University School of Medicine, 1975).

Coitus Interruptus (Withdrawal)

This technique requires that the man withdraw his penis from the woman's vagina before ejaculating. He must be careful not to ejaculate near her vagina: preejaculatory secretion, which may contain sperm, is capable of fertilizing the ovum. Further, this method requires a good deal of self-knowledge and control on the part of both partners. Ejaculation outside the vagina must be an acceptable sexual behavior. Clearly, this is not a very efficient method, but many couples limit and space their pregnancies by this method. Frustration and worry undoubtedly have a limiting effect on satisfaction derived from intercourse. For these reasons, it is advisable that the couple employ a second method of birth control.

Abstinence

Abstinence implies that sexual intercourse is not engaged in at any time during the woman's menstrual cycle. Because frustration is the usual side effect of this method, it is most applicable to the sexually inactive woman who has very strong convictions even when her partner tries to persuade her otherwise.

16

Permanent Methods
of Birth Control

Within a week of the operation, my determination to demonstrate that I hadn't lost anything important overcame my fear of hurting what I had left. Though somewhat restrained, we were reassured that I could still perform sexually to our satisfaction. A week later the sperm count in the doctor's office indicated we were "home free"—I was perfectly sterile, though not the least bit less virile.

My wife claims that I am more masculine than before the operation. I think I have gained a fuller confidence in knowing that my claim to manhood lies in personal characteristics other than my sperm count. If, for whatever reasons, I may have become a better husband, I know I have gained more in my wife. She has proof I no longer want her as a baby machine—I want and need more than that in a life partner. As a result, she has been able to plan her life without the fear that it will be interrupted again by a pregnancy and baby raising. She is now able to resume her career as a teacher, which in turn has made her a happier person, a more confident and capable mother, and a more responsible and interesting wife. Viva la vasectomy![1]

1. Kenneth H. Phillips, "One Couple's Decision" in *Foolproof Birth Control*, Lawrence Lader, ed. (Boston: Beacon Press, 1972), p. 31.

Status of Sterilization Today

There has been a marked increase in the demand for sterilization as a birth control method. In a little more than a decade, the number of sterilizations performed each year in the United States has grown from approximately 200,-000 to almost one million.[2] Most people desiring sterilization for contraceptive purposes are those who do not want to use another form of contraception for the rest of their fertile years.

Couples who obtain sterilizations seem to be very rational in their approach to contraception. The average couple has been married for over a decade. They have used a highly effective method of contraception prior to sterilization, have had all the children they wish to have (average 2.8), and have waited almost four years after the birth of their last wanted child before seeking sterilization. Since 1970, male vasectomies have been a more popular form of sterilization than female tubal ligations, probably because the operation is simple and inexpensive. In general, better educated couples prefer vasectomies, whereas the less educated choose tubal ligations, possibly reflecting sex role differences among social classes.[3]

The majority of people who have been sterilized report complete satisfaction with the operation. In one study of over 1,000 vasectomy cases, 73.1 percent reported that their sex life improved, while it remained the same for 25.4 percent, and deteriorated for only 1.5 percent. Requests for reversal are rare—approximately one for every thousand sterilizations performed.[4]

Although reversibility is possible, it is a costly, involved, and often unsuccessful venture. Therefore, sterilization procedures should be considered irreversible and should be elected only by those who desire a permanent

2. "The Better Way," *Redbook* (May 1973), p. 196.
3. Statistics compiled from "Contraceptive Sterilizations," *Family Planning Digest*, 2: 8 (March 1973).
4. Ibid. p. 45.

method of birth control. Continuing research is being carried on to develop temporary sterilization techniques for both men and women, but none as yet has been perfected.[5]

Counseling for Sterilization. Ideally, the counselor should make sure that neither party is being pressured into consent. In actual practice, the counselor may be put into the position of having to choose whether to support the desire for sterilization on the part of the woman when the man is reluctant to give consent. Particularly in instances of women who have had a number of children or who have health problems, such support may be necessary for the overall well-being of the family.

Consent of the spouse is not a legal requirement for voluntary sterilization. In an intact family unit, however, such consent should be sought in order to prevent possible misunderstanding. Frequently, a husband's or a wife's objections to the procedure may be based on fear resulting from inaccurate information regarding the physical and sexual results of sterilization.

Over the past several years there has been a growing interest in perfecting safe and simple methods of sterilization. This interest has been motivated in part by the growing demand for voluntary sterilization as a contraceptive method in this country. It has gained momentum as a result of the increased use of voluntary sterilization as a fertility check throughout the world, particularly in underdeveloped areas seeking to curb population growth. The most prevalent sterilization procedures currently used are discussed below.

Method of Male Sterilization

Vasectomy. There is general agreement that a vasectomy is a very simple and safe procedure. No body cavity

5. R.T. Ravenholt, "Overview of the Offices of Population, A.I.D., on Sterilization," in *Female Sterilization,* George Duncan, Richard Falb, and J. Joseph Speidel, eds., (New York: Academic Press, 1972), p. 1.

is entered and the operation takes only minutes to perform as an office procedure.

Procedure. A vasectomy involves making a small incision in the scrotum between the testicle and the groin. A small segment of the vas deferens, the tube which carries the sperm to the penis, is surgically removed. The ends are tied with absorbable surgical thread and the incision is stitched. The only pain involved is that caused by the injection of a needle into the vas prior to the surgery.

In most patients, a simple midline incision is all that is necessary, although two incisions may be made, one on each side. The surgical thread takes about two weeks to dissolve, and during this process scar tissue develops on each end of the severed vas, sealing it permanently[6]

A support strap is sometimes worn for a few days. Normal activities can be resumed almost at once (forty-eight to seventy-two hours after the procedure.) Sexual activity may be carried out within a few days when the skin incisions have had time to heal. There may be some discomfort if begun earlier.

Failure Rate. The failure rate[7] is now about one-half of

6. Ibid., p. 81.
7. Helen Edey, "Sterilization," in *Foolproof Birth Control,* ed. Lawrence Lader (Boston: Beacon Press, 1972) p. 44.

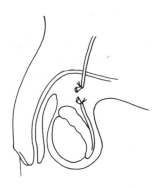

MALE STERILIZATION: VAS DEFERENS DIVIDED AND OCCLUDED

one percent. This figure is somewhat misleading, however, in that a much higher rate of pregnancy may result if unprotected intercourse is carried out within the first few weeks (or even months) following the procedure. The preoperative live sperm, largely dormant prior to ejaculation, can live for eight weeks or longer after a vasectomy.[8] The level of sexual activity largely determines when complete sterilization will be effected.

It is advisable for the man to take a semen specimen to the physician for examination before unprotected intercourse is attempted. The rare instances of recanalization of the vas usually occur in the first six months, and it is recommended that semen be reexamined every six weeks during that time.[9]

Complications. Vasectomy has no physiologic effect on a man's sexual performance or interest. Psychologically, it most often acts to increase libido and the level of sexual activity. Only rarely is activity decreased, usually by men who equate vasectomy with castration.[10] Complications associated with the procedure itself usually are minor and infrequent.

Methods of Female Sterilization

Over 100 surgical methods for female sterilization have been described in the literature.[11] It is clear from such a figure that the search for safe, effective, and acceptable means of female surgical sterilization has been diverse. Modern methods of female sterilization in practice in the United States today all bear two things in common. First, their goal is either blockage of the fallopian tube to prevent fertilization of the ovum, or removal of the uterus to

8. John Peel and Malcolm Potts, *Textbook of Contraceptive Practice* (Cambridge, England: Cambridge University Press, 1970), p. 167.
9. Alan Guttmacher, *Birth Control and Love*, (New York: Bantam Books, 1967) p. 167.
10. Peel and Potts, *Contraceptive Practice*, p. 163.
11. E.S.E. Hafez and T.N. Evans, *Human Reproduction* (New York: Harper and Row, 1973), p. 384.

accomplish the same purpose. Second, all methods of female sterilization require invasion of the abdominal cavity in some degree. Sterilization may be accomplished as an unavoidable result of surgical treatment for a variety of diseases of the female reproductive tract. The subject of sterilization should be discussed with any woman undergoing abdominal or pelvic surgery, so that sterilization may be performed at the same time if desired. Sterilization should not add any risk to abdominal surgical operations.

This section will focus on surgical procedures performed for purposes of sterilization only as a chosen method of contraception. Because such operations always necessitate the invasion of the abdominal cavity, all of the risks of infection, hemorrhage, and injury to adjacent organs inhere in such an operation The thrust of surgical technology in the field of female sterilization has been to limit these risks as much as possible by designing surgical approaches that reduce or eliminate the disturbance of other abdominal organs.

This goal can be accomplished by several methods. The first method is the timing of the sterilization procedure. Attention to timing is particularly important in relation to the patient who is about to undergo delivery, either vaginal or abdominal. If the patient is to be delivered by Cesarean section, tubal ligation adds no additional risk to the operative procedure. In patients who undergo vaginal delivery, because of the abdominal position of the uterus in the immediate postpartum period, the tubes are approachable through a very small abdominal incision without disturbance of the surrounding viscera. For patients who desire sterilization in the nonpregnant state, however, more problems exist; the uterus has assumed its low pelvic position and the pelvic organs, uterus, tubes, and ovaries are covered by the intestines. In these patients, the development of vaginal and endoscopic (laparoscope and culdoscope) procedures has limited the risk to the patient. The following table lists the methods of female sterilization in relation to time and technique.

TABLE 8   METHODS OF FEMALE STERILIZATION

I. Obstetrical
Postpartum tubal ligation following vaginal delivery
   Immediate (concurrent with delivery)
   Delayed (within seventy-two hours postpartum)
Cesarean section
   Tubal ligation
   Hysterectomy*

II. Interval (Interconceptional nonpregnant)
Tubal ligation
   Abdominal
   Vaginal (posterior colpotomy)
   Endoscopic procedure
      a. Laparoscopy
      b. Culdoscopy
Hysterectomy†
   Abdominal
   Vaginal

*†Still controversial from the standpoint of operative risk when done
  solely for sterilization.

This table is derived from Walter M. Wolfe, "Female Sexual Sterilization," Journal of the Kentucky Medical Association, 71:88 (February
1973).

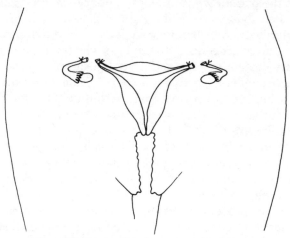

FEMALE STERILIZATION: FALLOPIAN TUBES DIVIDED AND OCCLUDED

Female sterilization for purposes of contraception most frequently involves blocking both fallopian tubes so that ova (eggs) cannot get from the ovaries to the uterus and the sperm cannot reach the ova. This operation is called a tubal ligation.

There are now over ten different tubal ligation procedures under experimentation or in use. The following are the three most used in the United States.

1. Tubal Ligation (The Pomeroy Technique)

This procedure is the one which has been used most frequently for a number of years.[12] This operation can be performed at the time of Cesarean section, in the immediate postpartum period after a vaginal delivery, or at any interval between pregnancies. Because the increased size of the uterus makes the operation easier, and it thus carries less risk, most physicians prefer the immediate postpartum period.

If the abdomen is already open, as it is in Cesarean section delivery, the procedure is done at that time. After normal vaginal delivery, the procedure can be performed through an abdominal incision. Frequently, this incision can be made through the already stretched umbilicus. As the abdominal wall and umbilicus shrink back to normal size after delivery, the incision disappears.

In the interval between pregnancies the operation may be done either through an abdominal incision or through the vagina (colpotomy).

Procedure. Through an appropriate incision either in the abdominal wall or through the posterior vaginal wall, or by colpotomy incision, a loop is tied in the midportion of the fallopian tube with an absorbable catgut suture. The segment between the two ends of the loop is removed. The catgut suture at the base of each loop is gradually absorbed by the body, leaving scar tissue at the two ends of the severed tube which lie about one and one-half in-

12. Guttmacher, *Birth Control and Love,* p. 162.

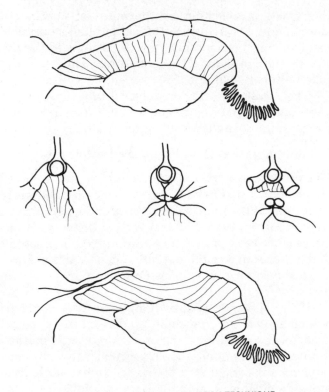

TUBAL LIGATION USING THE POMEROY TECHNIQUE

ches apart. General anesthesia is usually given, and there is a hospitalization of two to four days. If the operation is performed soon after the birth of a baby, little or no extra time is required for hospitalization.

Failure Rate— The failure rate of the technique depends upon timing. According to one authority, in the non-pregnant state there is a general failure rate of approximately 1 in 500 cases, in the postpartum period 1 in 200, and following Cesarean section 1 in 55 cases following the procedure.[13] Other statistics indicate much lower fail-

13. Ibid, p. 159.

ure rates. In over 29,000 tubal sterilizations reviewed by Allan E. Garb in 1957, the overall failure rate was 0.71%. There were 5,477 Pomeroy procedures in this group, with a failure rate of 0.40%.[14]

Complications. Tubal ligation carries more risk than male sterilization. A complication rate of 7 percent has been reported, mostly relating to minor wounds, and urinary tract infections. Serious complications or fatalities are rare, but can occur.[15]

Reversibility. Success in reversing this procedure so that the tubes can be reunited and pregnancy can result has been reported in less that 40 percent of the cases attempted. Further, because such repairs are complicated and costly and because the pregnancy rate is relatively low, tubal ligations should be considered permanent. Very few women, however, ever seek such reversals—perhaps 1 in 1000 who have had tubal ligations.[16]

2. Sterilization by Laparoscopy.

During the past ten years, the technique of laparoscopy has been added to the methods of sterilization. This technique is particularly applicable to the woman who chooses sterilization for contraception, but who is not pregnant or recently delivered (interconceptional). It is designed to avoid some of the risks, prolonged hospital care, and costs incurred with an abdominal or vaginal incision.

Procedure. Jaroslav F. Hulka provides the following description of the laparoscopic procedure: In the morning the patient is put to sleep in an operating room, and about two quarts of carbon dioxide (a clear gas that is safe to use with electric current) is put into the abdomen through a special needle that is inserted just below the navel. This

14. Allan E. Garb, "A Review of Tubal Sterilization Failures," *Obstetrical and Gynecological Survey*, 12:291 (1957).
15. Neuwirth, "Tubal Ligation, by Standard Techniques and the New Laparoscopic and Culdoscopic Approach," in *Foolproof Birth Control*, ed. Lawrence Lader, p. 93.
16. Ibid.

little opening in the skin is then made slightly larger (about as wide as a fingernail) and an instrument called a laparoscope, which is about as big around as a fountain pen, is inserted into the opening. With the use of this instrument, the surgeon can now see all the organs through the clear gas.

The tubes are between the womb and the ovaries and are smaller in size than an ordinary pencil. They are held with a special electrical instrument introduced through another, smaller opening lower in the abdomen. An electric current seals the tubes to prevent bleeding and the tubes are permanently divided. The instruments are removed, the carbon dioxide is let out, and the patient wakes up in a few minutes with two Band Aids over her navel and her lower abdomen.

Afterwards, women may have pains in their shoulders (from the carbon dioxide gas irritations) or pain where the instruments passed through the abdominal wall. These last a few hours and are usually gone in a day. Some may have a scratchy throat from the anesthesia. Most women are ready and eager to leave the hospital two to four hours after surgery, after the anesthesia wears off. Some are too tired from the anesthesia and excitement of surgery and appreciate an extra overnight rest. There is a discharge like a menstrual flow for a day or two. By the next day, most of these minor symptoms will be gone.[17]

Recently, Hulka has introduced the use of special clips which may be applied to the fallopian tube using the laparoscopic technique.[18] This technique removes the thermal burn risk inherent in the use of electrical cauterizing units within the abdominal cavity. Another method

17. Jaroslav F. Hulka, "Tying the Tubes with Laparoscopy," in *Foolproof Birth Control*, ed. Lawrence Lader (Boston: Beacon Press, 1972), pp. 97–98.
18. Jaroslav F. Hulka, et al. "Laparoscopic Sterilization with a Spring Clip, A Report of the First 50 Cases," *American Journal of Obstetrics & Gynecology*, 116:715 (July 1973).

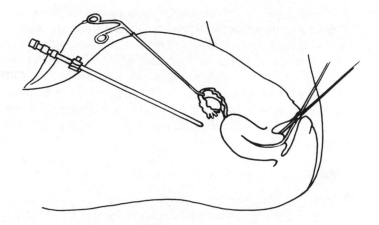

FEMALE STERILIZATION BY LAPAROSCOPY

which eliminates that danger is the use of the Fallop-Ring of Yoon, which has gained some popularity in this country.[19]

It should be noted that a one-incision technique has also been developed, and that local, rather than general, anesthesia is being used with increasing frequency.[20]

Failure Rate. Dr. Clifford R. Wheeless, of Johns Hopkins University, where much of the pioneering work with this method has been done, believes that the failure rate in which subsequent pregnancy results must be considered at 3 per 1,000. Actual followup of laparoscopic procedures performed at Johns Hopkins University Hospital Center, however, revealed only 1 subsequent pregnancy in 1,400 cases.[21]

19. In Bae Yoon and Theodore M. King, *The Journal of Reproductive Medicine*, 15:54 (November 1975).

20. Clifford Wheeless, "Outpatient Sterilization by Laparoscopy under Local Anesthesia in Less Developed Countries," in eds. *Female Sterilization* Duncan et al., (New York: Academic Press, 1972), p. 127.

21. Hulka et al., "Laparoscopic Sterilization."

Complications. The complication rate in laparoscopy is about 2 percent. Most of these complications are minor, such as minor skin burns and stitch abscesses. There are reports, however, of small but significant numbers of severe complications, such as bleeding or thermal burns of the bowels and other organs, which may require surgical correction. It is to be hoped that the introduction of the clip and ring techniques described above will eliminate these hazards.

3. Sterilization by Culdoscopy.

Culdoscopy has recently attracted much interest both here and abroad. Using this technique, the sterilization procedure is done through the vagina rather than the abdomen, thereby leaving no observable scars. It has the added advantage of often being done by local anesthesia on an outpatient basis.

Procedure. The patient is placed in a knee-chest position and anesthesia is administered. A trochar, or puncturing instrument, is used to perforate the upper rear portion of the vagina (posterior fornix). The opening is enlarged and a small telescope (culdoscope) is inserted, allowing the uterus, fallopian tubes, and ovaries to be seen. A tubal clamp is then inserted and guided under culdoscopic view. The tip of the clamp is used to grasp the midportion of the fallopian tube; the culdoscope is then removed, the clamped tube is brought into the vagina, where it is tied and cut. The two ends are then released and returned to their original position, and the procedure is repeated on the opposite side. A single suture covers the wound. The patient may be discharged in four to six hours. Full recovery takes a few days.

Failure Rate. The failure rate for sterilization ranges from zero to 5.2 percent. Failures are higher when the procedure is carried out for women who have not recently been pregnant.[22]

Complications. Complications have been reported to range from 3 percent to 13.3 percent.[23] There are major differences in complication rates in different parts of the world. India, where the operation is performed frequently, has the lowest complication rates, and the United States has among the highest. Anatomical differences, higher parity among Indian women, and less rigid reporting standards in India account for much of these differences. Infection and blood loss are the most prevalent complications.

22. Alfonso J. Gutierrez Najar, "Culdoscopy as an aid to Family Planning," in *Female Sterilization*, eds. Duncan et al., *Female Sterilization*, p. C42.

23. Brenton R. Lower, "Assessment of Sterilization Procedures," in *Female Sterilization*, eds. Duncan et al., p. C40.

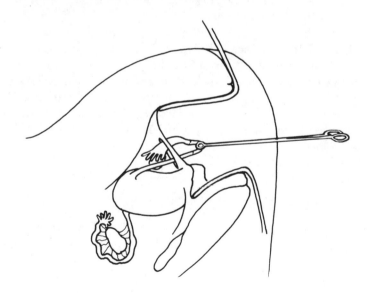

FEMALE STERILIZATION BY CULDOSCOPY

Hysterectomy.

Removal of the uterus, hysterectomy, is not usually done unless anomaly or disease are present—thus it is only secondarily a method of contraception. A hysterectomy is major surgery done under general anesthesia, and it requires several days of hospitalization. Full recovery is often slow. Usually the mouth of the uterus (the cervix) is also removed at the time of hysterectomy, because it can be the site of future carcinoma. The removal of both the uterus and the cervix is called a total hysterectomy; it can be performed by entering through either an abdominal incision or the vagina.

The ovaries are almost never removed at the time of hysterectomy unless it is absolutely essential, because they produce hormones important to the continued health of a woman. The removal of the ovaries (oophorectomy) is done only when medically indicated and is not a method of sterilization.[24]

Vaginal hysterectomy, in which access is effected through the vagina, is being used more frequently as a method of sterilization, particularly in women who may be at risk for gynecological diseases in the future. There is still medical controversy concerning the routine use of hysterectomy as a method of sterilization. The method clearly carries more operative risk than any of the methods of tubal ligation. Most physicians believe that sterilization is an inadequate reason for major surgery, especially because simpler effective techniques exist.[25]

The Social Worker's Role

The social worker should be aware of the rules and regulations of local clinics and hospitals regarding sterilization

24. Ibid.
25. Peel and Potts, *Textbook of Contraceptive Practice*, pp. 159–60.

procedures. Despite fairly liberal laws regarding voluntary sterilization, many hospitals have restrictive policies. Although the worker may choose to work to change regulations, knowing the policies is necessary if the worker is to make successful referrals.

It is essential that the worker make sure that the client understands the surgical procedure and that the goal is permanent sterility. If the tube or vas is properly surgically interrupted, it will not "grow together" spontaneously.

Many clients have questions which they are reluctant to ask; a clear explanation, even unsolicited, can relieve anxiety and doubt. Women as well as men fear that sterilization will harm their sexual activities; reassurances should be part of the counseling process. Many women believe that tubal ligations can only be performed following a delivery; many do not realize that they will still menstruate after the procedure. These and other misconceptions should be clarified by the counselor.

If sterilization is desired, but cannot be scheduled immediately, some other method of contraception should be offered. Contraceptive hormone injections are frequently given to women awaiting sterilization.

A patient undergoing any surgical procedure, including sterilization, must be legally capable of giving informed consent; that is, he or she must be of age and legally and mentally competent. If sterilization is considered without informed consent, clear legal permission, probably a court order, must be obtained.

Special legal questions regarding sterilization can be answered by contracting the Association for Voluntary Sterilization, or any of its branch offices (see Contraception and the Law).

Some doctors will suggest that the woman have a test to prove that the operation has been successful in closing the tubes. This test may be done by injecting carbon dioxide gas into the uterus through the cervix to determine if the tubes are blocked. Evidence of closure of the tubes may be obtained by injecting a special fluid into the uterus and taking an X-ray to demonstrate that the tubes are closed. Testing may reassure the patient that she is indeed sterile after the operation. It may also prevent the occasional unwanted pregnancy by warning the woman that there has been a failure so that she may take contraceptive precautions.

17

Abortion
Technology and
Counseling

I was completely muddled—and I had nowhere to go. But
friends kept helping and supporting—women supporting no decision, just me as I was. At about the point when I felt completely
spent and done in, I began to think about the responsibility of
making a decision. It became clear to me that my confusion was
a result of my unconscious desire to avoid making a real decision.
I couldn't come around to the reality of the situation. I had to
take on the responsibility of saying "I want to have this child and
I will accept that" or "I do not want another child and I must
accept the responsibility of aborting this fetus." I had to say that
I was real, that my life was real, and mine, and important. Those
feelings were very hard to come to. I don't think I believe in
them fully even now, but I did begin to think about myself in a
direct way, and I began to feel more sure of myself. There was
a certain strength in knowing that I could make a choice that was
mine alone and be entirely responsible to myself. It became very
clear to me that this was not the way to have a child, that in
thinking about the sanctity of life I had to think about the out-
come of my pregnancy, which would be a human being/child
that was not wanted. On the strength that I had begun to feel as
a woman I made the decision to have an abortion. There was no

194 | CONTRACEPTIVE TECHNOLOGY

decision of right or wrong or morality—it simply seemed the most responsible choice to make. It is still upsetting to me—the logic of it all—but somewhere within me it is still very clear, and I'm still very sure of that decision.[1]

Since the 1973 Supreme Court decision in regard to abortion, the availability of legal abortion in the United States has increased sharply. Careful monitoring of legal abortion systems in New York City and elsewhere since 1970, has indicated that abortions done in an approved medical setting are safer than full-time pregnancy and delivery. The Supreme Court decision had the effect of overturning restrictive abortion legislation in those states which had not already relaxed their abortion statutes. The statistical analysis entitled "Provisional Estimates of Abortion Needs and Services in the Year Following the 1973 Supreme Court Decision," states that there was an estimated need of 1.3 to 1.8 million abortions in the United States in the year 1974. Only 15 percent of public hospitals in the United States were performing abortions during the first part of 1974. More than 50 percent of the legal abortions done in 1974 were performed in abortion clinics. Abortion is generally available in metropolitan areas, but abortion services are difficult to find in rural areas and for the poor.[2]

In 1974, 763,476 legal abortions were reported by fifty states and the District of Columbia, to the Center for disease control. The national abortion rate increased from 196 abortions per 1,000 live births in 1973, to 242 in 1974. Seventy percent of the women receiving legal abortions were white; 73 percent were unmarried; 48 percent had no living children; 64 percent were under 25. In 1974,

1. Boston Women's Health Collective Course, *Our Bodies, Ourselves: A Book By and For Women* (New York: Simon & Schuster, 1973).
2. *Provisional Estimates of Abortion Needs and Services in the Year Following the 1973 Supreme Court Decision.* A report, prepared and published by the Alan Guttmacher Institute, a research and development division of Planned Parenthood Federation of America (New York: 1975), p. 86.

suction curettage accounted for 77 percent of all procedures; dilation curettage (12 percent); intrauterine saline instillation (8 percent); abdominal operations (1 percent). Eighty-seven percent underwent the procedure during the first 12 weeks of pregnancy. There were 24 deaths as the result of complications of legal abortions (3.1 per 100,-000 abortions); six deaths were known to be the result of illegal abortions; and eighteen deaths associated with spontaneous abortion. Suction curettage had the lowest rate of complications.[3]

Thus, the reality is that more and more women are utilizing abortion services. This is particularly true for low income women conceiving out-of-wedlock who had previously been denied access to legal abortion services because of their cost and inaccessibility.

There are several medical aspects of abortion that should be clear to the social worker and other practitioners who are counseling clients considering abortion. First, many women still believe abortion to be illegal and hence a very hazardous procedure. Clients should be informed that safe, legal abortion under medical conditions is available to them. Second, they should be informed that the earlier in pregnancy the abortion is performed, the simpler the procedure and the less likelihood that complications will arise. In this regard, it may be necessary for the counselor to develop contacts within the community to whom she can refer clients and expect reasonably prompt service. It would be preferable if such referrals were made personally by the counselor to the individual or clinic who will provide the services. This contact is of particular importance to those working in areas where abortion facilities may be difficult to find or perhaps unavailable.

The rate of complications resulting from abortion rises directly with the length of pregnancy. Thus, in the first

3. Center for Disease Control, *Abortion Surveillance Report, 1974,* (Atlanta, Ga.: U.S. Department of Health, Education and Welfare, 1976), pp. 1–3.

twelve weeks of pregnancy the incidence of minor complications is about 1 in 20 abortions, while serious complications occur in only 1 in 200 abortions. After twelve weeks, the incidence of complications increases three- to four-fold, due primarily to serious complications requiring hospitalization, blood transfusions, and additional surgical procedures.[4]

In addition, abortion in the second trimester (second three months of pregnancy) is considerably more expensive, requires two to three days of hospitalization, and may involve additional travel time in many areas of the country. Second trimester abortion is not available in many communities in which first trimester abortion may be relatively easy to obtain.

In 1973, the risk of death from pregnancy and childbirth, excluding abortion, was 14 per 100,000 live births, while the risk of death from legal abortion was 3.4 per 100,000 abortions. Two-thirds to three-quarters of these deaths occurred in abortions done after sixteen weeks of pregnancy.[5]

Women who are contemplating abortion require good abortion counseling to sort through their feelings and emotions about terminating a pregnancy. In the past, because abortion was illegal, abortion counseling was not provided. In the late 1960s, however, the techniques of abortion counseling were developed and put to effective use.

As legal abortions become more widespread so will pre-abortion and post-abortion counseling. The following discussion of abortion technology is designed to help the social worker gain information useful in developing skills in abortion counseling, a long neglected area in the social service provision.

4. Joint Program for the Study of Abortions (JPSA): Early medical complications, *Study in Family Planning*, 3:98 (June 1972).
5. Alan Guttmacher Institute Provisional Estimates of Abortion Needs, pp. 1–10.

ABORTION TECHNIQUES

There are various types of abortion techniques used today, including vacuum curettage; dilatation and curettage; and intraamniotic hypertonic saline procedure. Minisuction can be used for very early abortion or termination of suspected pregnancies. (See section on Post-intercourse Methods of Birth Control.)

Vacuum Curettage

Vacuum curettage (sometimes called the suction curettage, vacuum suction, uterine aspiration, or vacuum) can be done until the end of the twelfth week of pregnancy. A hollow tube is inserted into the uterus and a vacuum machine sucks out the implanted products of conception. This method can be safely performed in any properly equipped medical setting—such as a hospital, a clinic, or a doctor's office. During the early months of pregnancy, this method can be used with little blood loss, few risks of complications, little anesthesia, and a minimum of time and expense to the woman and the doctor.[6] The operation is so simple that it can be done by a paramedical specialist under the supervision of a doctor, if law permits.

Procedure. After the doctor has taken a thorough medical history and performed a physical examination of the patient, he can decide whether to do the abortion in a hospital, in his office, or in a clinic; his choice depends on the health of the woman and on the length of gestation (number of weeks of pregnancy). The doctor should also be aware of any adverse reactions to drugs or to local or general anesthesia in the woman's past.[7]

It is important for the doctor to test the woman for anemia, blood clotting time, and Rh blood factor. If the woman has Rh-negative blood, then she can develop an-

6. Donna Cherniak, and Allen Feingold, eds., *Birth Control Handbook* (Montreal: Journal Offset Inc., 1971), p. 40.
7. "Vacuum Aspiration," Health Organizing Collective of New York Women's Health and Abortion Project (New York: 1971), p. 2.

tibodies which will react against the fetal blood in future pregnancies. This reaction can cause many problems, including future neonatal death. If the woman has an injection of RhoGAM—immunoglobulin, derived from the blood of Rh-negative women who have been sensitized to the Rh factor. This injection will prevent sensitization if given within seventy-two hours after her abortion. She should not have any problems with future pregnancies.[8]

Many women prefer having the procedure done with local anesthesia to shorten their recovery time. For those women who prefer to be asleep during the abortion, a general anesthetic such as sodium pentathol is given by intravenous drip. These women will not be aware of anything during the procedure after this point.[9]

To stretch the vaginal walls, a speculum is inserted into the vaginal canal, in the manner employed in a routine examination. The speculum will keep the canal open throughout the entire operation. There is little pain associated with the insertion of the speculum. Next, a tenaculum is inserted to hold the cervix (the opening to the uterus) in place during the procedure. When the tenaculum first grasps the cervix there is a slight pinch.[10]

If the woman and the doctor decide to use a local anesthetic, a paracervical block is usually administered at this time. It provides enough anesthesia to block pain during the operation, and is less expensive and usually safer than using general anesthesia. It should be noted, however, that local anesthesia is associated with a higher risk of complications than general anesthesia among patients aborted by suction.[11] If a paracervical block is used, the anesthetic solution is injected in at least two points on the

8. Ibid., p. 3.
9. Ibid.
10. Ibid., pp 3–4.
11. *Abortion Surveillance Report: Legal Abortions, United States Annual Summary, 1971*, Center for Disease Control, Atlanta, Georgia (Washington, D.C.: Department of Health, Education, and Welfare, 1972).

cervix. There are very few nerve endings in the cervix, so the injection itself is not painful, and feelings from the cervix and the uterus are dulled.[12]

At this point, the doctor must dilate the cervical opening in order to have access to the uterus. Dilatation is usually accomplished by means of a series of specially designed rods. These rods vary in diameter from the size of a matchstick to the size of a piece of chalk and are passed into the cervical opening, one at a time. The small dilators are first inserted, and then progressively larger dilators are inserted gradually until the tip of the cannula, a disposable plastic tube, can fit into the opening; this part of the procedure usually requires about two minutes. Women have complained of cramps similar to menstrual cramps during the dilatation when no anesthesia is used; a woman who has had her cervix dilated previously, by births, miscarriages, or abortions, tends to have fewer cramps.[13]

In certain cases where the cervix is very small, as in very young girls, or is scarred as a result of previous surgery or deliveries, or in more advanced pregnancies (longer than twelve weeks), the doctor may choose to utilize the Lamineria Tent for slow dilatation of the cervix over a period of hours. This instrument is a sterilized rod made of a special seaweed which has the capacity to swell to ten times its normal diameter, with the absorption of body fluids. It is inserted in the cervix under sterile conditions, eight to twelve hours prior to the procedure, and the dilatation of the cervix proceeds slowly and painlessly over this period of time. When properly used, this may eliminate entirely the requirement for dilatation of the cervix at the time of the abortion.[14]

Once the cervix is dilated, the cannula can be inserted. The cannula is attached to plastic tubing several feet long,

12. Cherniak and Feingold, *Birth Control Handbook*, p. 40.
13. Ibid.
14. Ralph W. Hale, and Ronald J. Pion, Laminaria: "An Underutilized Clinical Adjunct," *Clinical Obstetrics and Gynecology*, 15:840–45 (September 1972).

which in turn is connected to collection bottles. When the cannula is in place, the physician turns on the suction machine and gently moves the cannula around to reach all parts of the uterus. He watches to be sure that the fetal and placental tissues are sucked into the collection bottles. The physician then inserts a spoon tipped instrument called a curette and gently scrapes the uterine lining to be sure that all the material has been removed by the vacuum. The operation takes five to ten minutes to perform.[15] Bleeding similar to a normal menstrual period will last from one day to three weeks after an abortion; it should not be confused with hemorrhaging. The woman will usually have her next menstrual period three to seven weeks after the abortion.[16]

If a woman has been given general anesthesia she will need two hours' recovery time. During this time she may also experience nausea, vomiting, or disorientation. The recovery time from a local anesthesia is shorter.[17]

Reactions. It is difficult to generalize about reactions to the procedure, because women react to pain and discomfort in many different ways. Reactions seem to depend not only on physical factors, but also on psychological factors. A woman may have a more traumatic experience if she does not want an abortion, but chooses to proceed because of financial, social, or family pressures. If she feels a great deal of guilt about having an abortion, she may have more physical problems. Many women want an abortion, but are frightened by the stories they have heard about "back-alley-butchers;" these women also seem to have additional problems because they are tense and worried about the procedure. If a woman is given local anesthesia it is recommended that she have a reassuring person by her side throughout the procedure to talk to her, explain the procedure as it progresses, or just hold her hand. It is also

15. Ibid., p. 40.
16. Ibid.
17. "Vacuum Aspiration," Health Organizing Collective, p. 5.

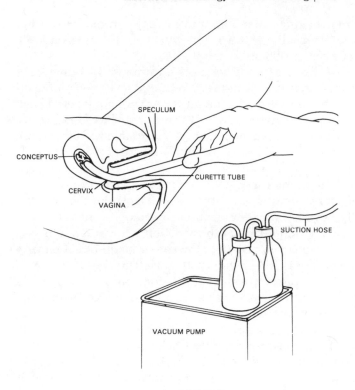

SPECULUM

CONCEPTUS

CURETTE TUBE

CERVIX

VAGINA

SUCTION HOSE

VACUUM PUMP

VACUUM CURETTAGE

important that the doctor performing the procedure be supportive.

Complications. It is estimated that 1 to 4 out of 1,000 women will experience hemorrhaging after an abortion.[18] Hemorrhaging means loss of more than one pint of blood. It can be caused by perforation of the uterine wall by one of the surgical instruments. Most perforations of the uterus are small and will heal by themselves; however, if the perforation is large, other internal organs may be damaged as well as the uterus. The patient will experience

18. Ibid.

hemorrhaging, infection, and possibly other danger signals. Perforation of the uterus will occur in approximately 2 of every 1,000 abortions.[19]

If a woman has large clots and heavy bleeding, it is possible that not all the fetal material has been removed from the uterus or that the uterus has not contracted back to the prepregnant size.[20] If the doctor has failed to remove all of the fetal or placental material in the uterus, the woman will need to be hospitalized for a dilatation and curettage (D and C).

If a woman experiences nausea, vomiting, heavy cramping, or a temperature above 100 degrees F., she may have an infection. Causes of infection include: nonsterile technique during the abortion; a lower resistance to infection after an abortion; the spread of an infection present before the abortion; material left in the uterus after the abortion; or introducing infection into the vagina by having intercourse, douching, and so forth, before the uterus has healed.[21]

It is most important to the woman's health and possibly her life that she seek medical help immediately if any of these danger signals arise after an abortion. The earlier the woman seeks medical help for complication, the easier it is to solve the problem.

Post-abortion. A woman may resume her normal activity within several hours after a vacuum curettage. She will be cautioned, however, against douching, using vaginal deodorants, taking tub baths, or having oral, manual, or genital intercourse for two to four weeks after the operation, to prevent any infection from being introduced into the uterus. Ergotrate is a drug sometimes given to women to help the uterus contract to its normal size and muscle tone. This drug can reduce the possibility of hemorrhaging or infections.[22] The contraction caused by Ergotrate may cause some cramping pain.

19. Ibid.
20. Ibid., p. 5–6.
21. Ibid., p. 6–7.
22. Center for Disease Control, *Abortion Surveillance Report*, p. 19.

Dilation and Curettage

The dilatation and curettage (D and C) method was used widely until vacuum curettage came into being. It is still used for abortions between the twelfth and fifteenth weeks of pregnancy. In some cases, the vacuum curettage is not available or the doctor prefers the D and C and so performs an early abortion with this technique. Approximately 21 percent of all abortions are done by dilatation and curettage.[23]

Procedure. The procedure for a D and C is the same as with vacuum curettage—medical history, check for Rh factor, pelvic examination, and cervical dilatation—but it is done in a hospital and the woman is given a general anesthesia. When the cervix is dilated, a curette is introduced into the uterus; the curette is used to scrape fetal and placental material off the uterine walls. Ovum (ring) forceps are then used to remove the fetal and placental material from the uterus.[24]

Dilatation and curettage may be combined with vacuum aspiration. In such procedures, ovum (ring) forceps are inserted alternating with the cannula and vacuum suction to remove fetal and placental material. The uterine lining is then checked with a large curette to insure that all fetal tissue has been removed. This procedure takes ten to fifteen minutes, requires at least an overnight stay in the hospital, and involves a greater loss of blood than simple use of the vacuum curettage.[25]

Post-abortion. A woman who undergoes a D and C will be given the same postabortion instructions as those given in the case of the vacuum curettage—no douching, or tub baths, and so forth—and she will be told to watch for the same danger signs. It will take the patient a little longer to recover from a D and C than from a vacuum curettage, and the procedure is more expensive.

23. Cherniak and Feingold, *Birth Control Handbook*, p. 41.
24. Ibid.
25. Ibid.

IntraAmniotic Hypertonic Saline and Prostaglandin

Saline injection can be performed after the sixteenth week of pregnancy counting from the first day of the patient's last menstrual period, although some physicians prefer to wait until later. The procedure cannot be performed until this time because the amniotic sac cannot be located until then. Before the procedure is performed, a complete medical history of the woman should be taken. She should be given several blood and urine tests to make sure that no complications have arisen involving the lungs and heart. If the woman has an Rh-negative blood factor, as mentioned earlier in the section on vacuum curettage, she should be given RhoGAM within seventy-two hours after the saline procedure has been completed.[26]

Recently, a substance called prostaglandin has been used to replace saline in midtrimester (over sixteen weeks) abortions. Prostaglandin does not require withdrawal of fluid, eliminates some of the risks involved with saline infusion, and has a shorter aborting time (less than eighteen hours after injection).[27]

In addition to saline and prostaglandin, the woman may also receive a hormone called oxytocin by continuous flow into a vein in her arm. This substance reinforces the labor contractions and speeds up the abortion process.[28]

Some hospitals also use the Lamineria Tent to help dilate the cervix to further shorten the time between injection and abortion.[29]

26. "Saline Abortions," Health Organizing Collective of New York Women's Health and Abortion Project (New York: 1971), pp. 3–8.
27. William E. Brenner, et al., "Induction of Therapeutic Abortion with Antra-Amniotically Administered Prostaglandin F_2 a.," *American Journal of Obstetrics and Gynecology*, 116:923–30 (1973).
28. Tibor Engel, et al. "Mid-Trimester Abortions Using Prostaglandin F_2a, Oxytocin and Lamineria," *Fertility and Sterility Journal*, 24:-565–67 (August 1973).
29. Phillip G. Stubblefield, et al. "Pretreatment with Laminaria Tents Before Mid-Trimester Abortion with Intra-Amniotic Prostaglandin F_2a," *American Journal of Obstetrics and Gynecology*, 118:284–85 (January 1974).

Procedure. To perform a saline injection, a small area about three to six inches wide just below the navel is numbed by a local anesthetic. A long needle is passed through the skin, through the abdominal wall, through the uterine wall, and into the amniotic sac. The physician withdraws some amniotic fluid (water); the amount withdrawn depends on the physician's preference. Sometimes the needle is then replaced by a fine plastic tubing. The plastic tubing reduces the risk of dislodging the needle. Through the same needle or plastic tubing, the doctor will inject or drip a 20 percent salt solution into the amniotic sac. Special care is taken to ensure that the saline solution goes into the amniotic sac and not into the bloodstream or the uterine wall. The salt solution inactivates the placenta and also causes the uterus to expand. The woman will go into labor within a few hours.[30]

Contractions usually begin five to fifteen hours after the injection. The contractions, discomfort, and expulsion of the fetus are usually not as painful as giving birth to a full-term baby. Generally, the amniotic sac will break, and a salty liquid is expelled. After this expulsion the contractions usually become harder and closer together. General anesthesia is sometimes given once contractions begin so that the woman will feel nothing. After eight to fifteen hours of labor the fetus is expelled. On the average, the abortion is completed twenty-eight hours but may range from eight to seventy-two hours after the saline injection.[31]

Post-abortion. Usually a hospital will keep a woman for twenty-four hours after she aborts; doctors will often give the patient antibiotics or some other kind of medication following this type of abortion.[32] She will probably have bleeding for several weeks. A woman can expect to menstruate four to eight weeks after the saline abortion. She

30. "Saline Abortions," Health Organizing Collective, pp. 3–8.
31. Ibid., p. 4.
32. Ibid.

should not douche, use vaginal sprays, take tub baths, or have oral, genital, or manual intercourse for two to four weeks after the abortion.[33]

Complications. During the saline injection the woman is awake so that she can tell the doctor of any unusual symptoms—such as numbness, pain, headache, or faintness—all of which can be caused by a misdirected injection. If the salt solution is injected into a blood vessel, there may be serious consequences. If contractions do not begin, a second saline injection is required to start them. Sometimes a woman will expel the fetus, but some of the placenta will remain in the uterus. A simple D and C can be done to solve this problem. The problem of hemorrhaging is not as common as with the D and C or vacuum curettage; however, the problem of infection is higher, and the woman must be cautioned to watch for signs indicating infection.[34]

The basic principles of abortion counseling have been covered in Chapter 11 and need not be repeated here.

33. Ibid.
34. Ibid.

A Final Note

This book is not only about counseling techniques, contraceptive technology, and information dissemination—it is also concerned with helping people plan their own lives, and bring children into this world who will be desired and cherished. The information in this book is for those who want to help women in this endeavor of "happy mothers, happy babies."

To accomplish this end, those in the helping professions must be knowledgeable about birth control, infertility counseling, and sexual problems. They must learn to accept themselves and their own sexual predilections. They must learn to be accepting of others and their predicaments. Preconceived judgments must be put to rest while they concentrate on the thinking, feelings, and problems of those they strive to help.

Family planning and sexual relations are central issues which almost every individual faces, and, therefore, are concerns which confront social workers continually. If the caring professional will take the time and effort to become familiar with the knowledge and skills needed as a facilitation in helping people in these areas, there will be a broad range of benefits, both to client and to worker.

There is no formula—but knowledge and skills can go a long way in providing the guidance which clients are seeking. Without knowledge, there is no adequate counseling, without understanding there is no reasonable course of action. The overall philosophy of this book has been that people have the right to knowledge and support in determining their own destinies to the greatest possible extent. In order to help others become independent, workers have the responsibility to become knowledgeable themselves and to serve as resource professionals in helping their clients in these most basic and important decisions of their lives.

Index

Abortion counseling, 44, 112–117, 193–
196
 adolescents, 124
 alternative choices, 114–115
 conditions and methods for, 113–114
 confidentiality, 114
 death rate, 196
 federal laws, 11–12, 15–17
 followup technique, 116–117
 needs and services, 194–195
 post-abortion counseling, 116–117,
196
 presumptive abortions, 161
 responsibility of client, 115–116
 responsibility of counselor, 112–113,
115–116
 attitudes and biases, 112–113
 sources of information, 18
 Supreme Court decision (1973), 11–
12, 16–17, 194
 types of abortions, 115–116
Abortion techniques, 197–206
 complications, 195–196, 201–202
 dilatation and curettage, 203
 hemorrhaging after abortion, 201
 intra-amniotic hypertonic saline and
prostaglandin, 204–206
 Rh-negative blood factor, 197–198,
204
 saline injections, 204–206
 vacuum curettage, 197–202

Abstinence method of birth control,
173, 175
Adolescent counseling, 121, 132–137
 access to contraceptives, 12–13, 124–
125
 parental consent, 13
 basic guidelines, 136–137
 communication problems, 132–133
 contraceptive counseling, 18, 132–
137
 guilt feelings, 134
 helping relationship, 132–133
 "I want to be pregnant" syndrome,
135
 "It can't happen to me" syndrome,
134
 legal aspects, 12–13
 "moral" teen-age syndrome, 133–134
 parental consent requirements, 12–
14
 referral problems, 135–136
 resistances to contraception, 133–
135
 sexual victim pattern, 134–135
 sterilization, 13–15
 welfare recipients, 18
Adolescent sexuality, 121–131
 abortions, 124
 approval of pre-marital sex, 127
 attitudes toward sex, 127, 131
 blacks and, 129–131

209